BARCELONA

The Buildings of Europe

BARCELONA

Christopher Woodward

Photographs by Carmel Lewin

MANCHESTER UNIVERSITY PRESS

Manchester and NewYork

Distributed exclusively in the USA and Canada by St. Martin's Press

Author's acknowledgements

I should like to thank the following people who offered valuable advice, help and criticism: Iain Borden; Peter Buchanan; Mark Bury, my first guide; James Cummins, Professor Emeritus of Spanish at University College London; and Richard Veith who went there first.

Copyright © Christopher Woodward 1992

Published by
Manchester University Press
Oxford Road, Manchester M13 9PL, UK
and
Room 400, 175 Fifth Avenue, New York,
NY 10010, USA

Distributed exclusively in the USA and Canada by
St Martin's Press, Inc., 175 Fifth Avenue,
New York, NY 10010, USA

British Library cataloguing in publication data
A catalogue record for this book is available from the British Library

Library of Congress cataloguing in publication data applied for

ISBN 0 7190 3514 7 hardback
ISBN 0 7190 3515 5 paperback

Printed in Great Britain by
Biddles Ltd, Guildford and King's Lynn

Typography by Nick Loat

How to use this guide

There are about 230 entries—buildings, squares, parks, engineering structures—arranged chronologicaly. Each entry has a reference number followed by an uppercase letter. This letter is the key to one of the twelve 2.5 kilometre squares into which the general map of Barcelona on pages 154–155 is divided. Section J includes the area of the Ciutat Vel and the Parc della Ciutadella and has its own enlarged map on pages 156–157. This is further divided into twelve squares each referenced by a lowercase letter. Where appropriate, the nearest metro 'M' or Ferrocarril 'F' station is given for each entry.

There are two further lists: the first is a selection of noteworthy interiors: these have reference numbers starting at 300 and are indicated on the maps with an open circle. The second, 'Excursions', lists significant buildings outside Barcelona. These are by architects who practised mainly in Barcelona or which otherwise contribute to its architectural history. The excursions have reference numbers starting at 400.

The visitor to Barcelona is well served with information. Maps of the metro and bus routes can be obtained for example from Sants station. The Ajuntament's tourist office at Gran via des Corts Catalanes, 658 can provide information about the opening hours of those buildings whose interiors can be visited, and it frequently publishes small guides to particular architectural topics.

The inclusion of a building in this guide does not mean that its grounds or interior are accessible. Please respect the privacy of those living or working in the buildings mentioned.

Contents

View from Tibidabo; in the foreground, the Fabra Observatory 114

Introduction

Barcelona has the sea, ships and sailors, and the palm and pine trees, of other Mediterranean ports like Genoa, Marseille and Malaga. But since its foundation the city has undergone a small number of very sudden transformations, and for the visitor its streets, squares, buildings and architecture continue to offer extraordinarily vivid evidence of these changes. The modern city of about two million people lies on a narrow coastal plain, its boundaries defined by the sea; by two rivers, the Llobregat to the south-west and the Besós to the north-east; and by the small mountain range of Collserola, offspring of the Pyrenees, including Tibidabo, to the north-west. The mountain of Montjuïc rises steeply from the sea on the south-west and separates the residential city from the modern port and manufacturing areas beyond.

Roman Barcelona

The Romans had occupied and ruled the Iberian peninsula for two hundred years before establishing, in the second century, the town of Barcino next to the sea. Its site straddled a southern bypass off the road (the via Augusta) between the present cities of Girona and Tarragona, the latter the capital of a Roman province. Evidence of their settlement is visible today in the substantial remains of the circuit of walls built in the fourth century 1, and in the few columns of the Temple of Augustus 1. Modern archaeological work continues to expose the walls by demolishing medieval and later accretions, most recently at the south-west corner of the circuit.

The Visigoths and Moors

After the fall of the Western Roman Empire in the fifth century the Visigoths, originally from Scandinavia, occupied much of the Iberian peninsula from the north. At first they made Barcelona their capital, but later moved this to Toledo, from where they ruled for the next three hundred years. The occupation of the peninsula by Arabs and Muslim Berbers from north Africa (later called 'Moors')

Introduction

started in 711, but although they briefly occupied Barcelona, the extent of their rule was bounded to the north-east by the Garraf mountains—there are no Moorish buildings or their ruins in Barcelona. During the ninth and tenth centuries the Franks, one of the Christian powers gradually driving the Moors westward, ruled Barcelona as a March governed by hereditary Counts, and the city had no part in the continuing battles of the Christian Reconquest which led to the capture of Toledo in 1085.

The Kingdom of Barcelona, capital of Catalonia

In the eleventh century, the Counts Berenguer Ramon I and Ramon Berenguer I 'el Vell' established the independence of Barcelona and its newly-named province Catalonia from the Franks. Subsequent Counts amalgamated other provinces through marriage, and by the end of the twelfth century the Count-Kings of Barcelona and Aragón ruled Catalonia, Aragón, and eastward across the Pyrenees as far as what is now French Provence. Jaume I 'the Conqueror' (1213–76) united the four kingdoms of Catalonia, Valencia, Aragon and Majorca. By the fourteenth century, Barcelona had extended her Mediterranean trading empire as far west as Athens, whose Duchy was won from Byzantium, and it included the islands of Sicily and Corsica. Trade with all the Mediterranean countries expanded, and the beginnings of modern banking were established in the Llotja **16**, one of Europe's first purpose-built exchanges. It was during this century and in the reigns of Jaume II 'the Just' (1291–1327) and Pere III 'the Ceremonious' (1336–87) that most of the extant Gothic buildings in the Ciutat Vella were constructed to provide settings for the institutions of a prosperous medieval city: the secular halls including the Saló de Tinell **13**, the Cathedral **7**, the large churches of Santa Maria del Pi **9** and Santa Maria del Mar **11**, and the monastery at Pedralbes **10**. The dockyards, Drassanes **15**, begun in 1255, were expanded in the middle of the fourteenth century, and continued to be extended until late into the next.

A new circuit of walls was built beyond that of the Romans, its south-western side a continuous rampart at the edge of the river which ran to the sea along the line of the modern Ramblas. Development was limited by decree to the town within the walls, and only religious and hospital buildings and theatres were allowed or required to be built outside them. The consequence was the very dense medieval city, some of whose buildings, and much of whose street pattern, later cut through by the straight streets of the nineteenth century, is still visible. The last military conquest by the Kingdom of Barcelona, in the fifteenth century, was that of Naples. But the fall of Constantinople to the Turks in 1453 ended Barcelona's maritime dominance of much of the Mediterranean and led to an immediate decline in her trade.

The marriage of King Ferdinand and Queen Isabel in 1469 united Spain's two largest and most powerful Iberian kingdoms of Aragón, which then included Catalonia, and Castile. The political histories of Barcelona and Spain become aligned. In 1492, the last Moors were expelled from the peninsula, and Cristobal Colom (Christopher Columbus) set sail for the Indies. On his return in 1493 he was received by Ferdinand and Isabel in Barcelona's Saló del Tinell **13**. This event symbolically launched Spain's American empire but continued the erosion of Barcelona's economic importance. Seville, to the south west, became the chief port from which colonial expeditions left and to which their booty returned.

The sixteenth and seventeenth centuries

In the sixteenth century, under Charles I, the Spanish crown was united with that of Austria with Madrid as capital, and Barcelona was reduced to the capital of a small state or province, the Generalitat of Catalonia, and stripped of many of its medieval rights of self-government. To house Madrid's governor, the Viceroy, between 1549 and 1557 the Palau del Lloctinent **23** was built next to the earlier royal palace. One hundred years later, the first castle was built on the summit of Montjuïc during the Spanish Wars of Succession.

The earliest farmhouse, or masia, recorded here is from 1610, the masia Torre Rodona **24**. Several others have survived, including **46** and **47**. Formerly standing in their estates and now usually engulfed by the development of modern Barcelona, they present a long-lasting building type. All have a pyramidal composition of a central three-storey hipped-roofed pavilion flanked by two-storey wings.

The eighteenth century

J.B.Trend in *The Civilization of Spain* suggests that 'Spain had no seventeenth century and no eighteenth century in the ordinary European sense', and the Bourbon rule of Spain in the eighteenth century has left little evidence of civil architectural activity in Barcelona. Its chief monuments are military.

In 1714 one of Catalonia's periodic rebellions against Castilian rule was put down by Philip V. The siege of Barcelona by the Duke of Berwick lasted for eleven months, and the city's casualties are commemorated in the memorial park Fossa de les Moreres to the south of the church of Santa Maria del Mar **11**. The city was put under the military rule of a Governor, the medieval corporations dissolved, and

Introduction

the construction of the enormous fort, the Ciutadella **31**, begun on the site of the Barri Ribera in the north eastern corner of the city. The ramparts were finished in 1727, and the fort was then equipped for the military with the buildings of a self-contained town. The architect of these buildings, Pròsper de Werboom, proposed housing the former inhabitants of the Barri in a new quarter on the flat and vacant land to the east of the fort, and in 1751 the new suburb of Barceloneta **36** was begun. This was the first large planned extension of the city outside its medieval walls, and was laid out on an extraordinarily elongated grid. The military supervision of Barcelona was completed in the south by the new ramparts to the castle on Montjuïc built between 1751 and 1779.

The Rambla (from the Arabic for 'sand', *rami*) was originally a seasonal river bed used as a road and it had provided the eastern boundary to the medieval walls. In the last quarter of the eighteenth century the walls along its length were demolished and the land on either side of the road reordered by the military engineer de Cermeño. On the west side, the Palau de la Virreina **41**, begun in 1772, and the Casa March de Reus **43** and the Palau Moja **40** on the opposite side were among the aristocratic palaces built in the 1770s to take advantage of the spacious sites fronting the broad new street. The end of the century saw the building of institutions: the first Customs House, the Duana Vella **45**, and a new theatre, since rebuilt as the Teatre Principal **44**.

Industrialisation

The first industries in Spain were established in Barcelona in the last two decades of the eighteenth century, when the wool crafts were replaced by an efficient but small-scale textile industry promoted by the development of colonial American cotton plantations (the woollen industry continued to be concentrated outside Barcelona in Sabadell and Tarrassa). Other less important industries grew up, including hosiery manufacture, paper processing, printing, and the fabrication of light machinery. New workers, immigrants from southern France and Italy, and from Catalonia's rural hinterland, swelled the population, and Catalan became their common language. They were housed mainly within the confines of the medieval walls, and to accommodate them much of the city was rebuilt at increasingly higher densities. Industrialisation continued during the first half of the nineteenth century and further increases in population gave rise to the appalling urban conditions catalogued by Cerdà and others: malnutrition, squalid housing, civil unrest, pollution and disease, this last evidenced in a series of epidemics of yellow fever and cholera (the last outbreak of yellow fever occurred in 1870 and killed over a thousand people). Between 1818 and 1860, Barcelona's population more than doubled from 88,000 to 190,000 and it became and remains one of the densest cities in Europe. In 1859 there were 859 people per hectare, over twice the density of Paris and ten times London's 86. Both the government in Madrid and the Barcelona authorities decided that the city needed reordering and that a plan for its expansion was required. They determined that the plain on which the medieval city stood surrounded by the villages of Sarrià, Gràcia and Sant Andreu i Horta had to be colonised.

The *Eixample*, the Pla Cerdà

Ildefons Cerdà i Sunyer was born in 1815 in Centellas outside Barcelona. He trained as architect in Barcelona and qualified as a civil engineer in Madrid. From 1849, when he inherited the family estates, he practised independently as a student and critic of social conditions, statistics, cartography and urbanism. In 1859 he was invited by the government in Madrid to submit proposals for the expansion of Barcelona. At the same time, however, the Barcelona authorities had organised their own competition for proposals, and the publication of these coincided with Madrid's approval of Cerdà's plan. The political 'Battle of the Expansion Zone' between the central and municipal governments and between public and private development was started, and has erupted throughout Barcelona's history ever since.

Cerdà proposed nothing less than a complete transformation of the political and physical views of what a city was. His main principle was that of co-operation rather than competition: each citizen was to be guaranteed basic housing standards of space, daylight and air, and to have easy access to services and public transport. Each part of the city was to have a similar organisation: different social classes would not be identified with particular zones or urban patterns. The pattern of circulation would be regular, with only two classes of road, and excessive concentrations of particular functions or services were to be avoided. Densities of development were to be low and evenly spread.

The plan proposed a square grid of roads and blocks, its warp and weft like the textiles which had become the source of Barcelona's industrial strength, and, as Cerdà noted, similar to the pattern of Spanish colonial towns. The roads were set out at centres of 133 metres and all were to be twenty metres wide except for the five main arteries which could have widths of up to fifty metres. The central road running south-east to north-west, parallel to the coast, now the Gran via de les Corts Catalanes, divides the city into two and provides a long axis. The short axis is marked by the passeig Sant Joan. Crossing the grid on diagonals were the

Introduction

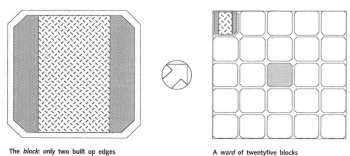

The *block*: only two built up edges

A *ward* of twentyfive blocks

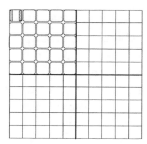

A *district* of four wards

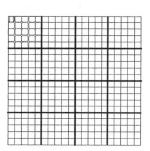

A *sector* of sixteen wards

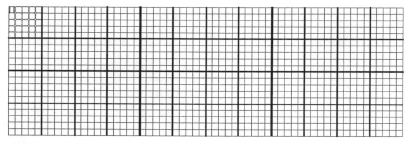

An *urban region* of three sectors

The three sectors of the Pla Cerdá

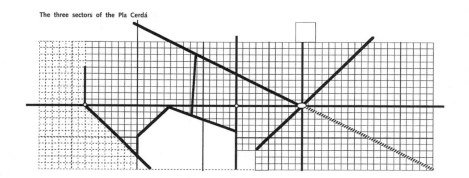

road to Tarragona to the south-west, now the avinguda Diagonal, and the road to Girona to the north, the avinguda de la Meridiana. The last two cross the Gran Via at what is now the plaça de les Glòries Catalanes (whose present confused junction is, through work started in 1990, being geometrically reorganised into a gigantic elliptical roundabout which will stare up from the modern plan of Barcelona like a huge eye).

The administrative and social units of the city (illustrated on the opposite page) would be formed of multiples of the basic block: a ward would be a group of five by five, or twenty-five blocks, with its own local centre; a district would consist of four of these wards. Sectors of twenty by twenty blocks would be formed of four districts. The theoretical application of the grid to the plain of Barcelona, a rectangle of sixty by twenty blocks, would have constituted twelve 'districts', one of which would have been the old city, or three 'sectors' each of twenty by twenty blocks. Each new sector was served by at least one of the main arteries passing through it, and the Ciutat Vella was to be ventilated by extending and cutting three of the new roads through it. Only one of these was eventually built: the via Laietana which extended south-west from the carrer Pau Claris.

The corners of each block were chamfered to allow for easy turning movements for vehicles, and to provide local urban concentrations. Cerdà proposed an even and very low density for the development of each block: a coverage of only about one-third of the sites, the rest planted with trees. With building heights of a maximum of sixteen metres, and of reasonable depth, at most three edges of any block would be occupied, and the chamfered corners were the only place at which frontages would be fully built up.

Cerdà's plan was adopted by the Madrid government and immediately implemented. In spite of an economic slump in 1866, during the next twenty years much of the infrastructure, streets, services and sewers, was put in place. Although Cerdà himself designed a model building on the corner of one of his blocks at carrer del Consell de Cent **59**, few of his detailed proposals were implemented by the city. As they were finished, the serviced sites were sold to speculators for development at much higher densities than he had suggested, and without the open spaces essential to his vision. Cerdà continued to write and publish, but his attempts to combine the reform of society with the reform of the city were finally rejected and after his death in voluntary exile in 1876, his reputation was systematically destroyed. His legacy is the grid of the *Eixample*, unique in Europe, which provided an ideal setting for the buildings commissioned

The architects of *Modernisme*

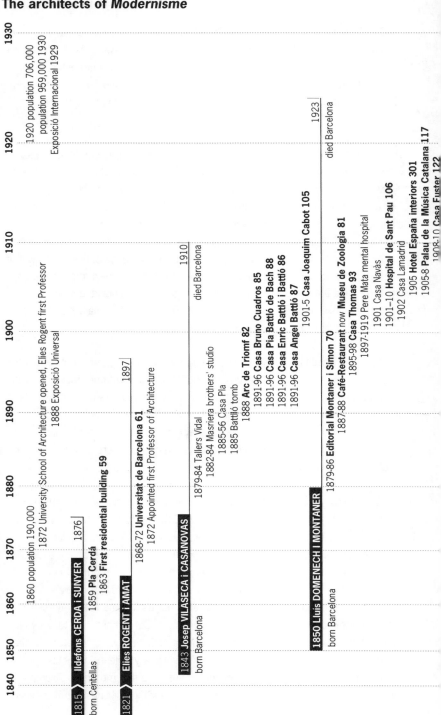

1840 | 1850 | 1860 | 1870 | 1880 | 1890 | 1900 | 1910 | 1920 | 1930

1860 population 190,000
1920 population 706,000
population 959,000 1930
Exposició Internacional 1929

1872 University School of Architecture opened, Elies Rogent first Professor
1888 Exposició Universal

1815 **Ildefons CERDA i SUNYER**
born Centellas
1859 **Pla Cerdà**
1863 **First residential building 59**
1876

1821 **Elies ROGENT i AMAT**
1868-72 **Universitat de Barcelona 61**
1872 Appointed first Professor of Architecture
1897

1843 **Josep VILASECA i CASANOVAS**
born Barcelona
died Barcelona
1910
1879-84 Tallers Vidal
1882-84 Masriera brothers' studio
1885-56 Casa Pla
1885 Battlló tomb
1888 **Arc de Triomf 82**

1891-96 **Casa Bruno Cuadros 85**
1891-96 **Casa Pia Battló de Bach 88**
1891-96 **Casa Enric Battló i Battló 86**
1891-96 **Casa Angel Battló 87**
1901-5 **Casa Joaquim Cabot 105**

1850 Lluis DOMENECH I MONTANER
born Barcelona
died Barcelona
1923
1879-86 **Editorial Montaner i Simon 70**
1887-88 **Café-Restaurant** now **Museu de Zoología 81**
1895-98 **Casa Thomas 93**
1897-1919 Pere Mata mental hospital
1901 Casa Navàs
1901–10 **Hospital de Sant Pau 106**
1902 Casa Lamadrid
1905 **Hotel España interiors 301**
19058 **Palau de la Música Catalana 117**
1908-10 **Casa Fuster 122**

born Reus

1878-85 **Casa Vicens 68**

1883-93 crypt, Sagrada Família

1884-87 **Gatehouse & pavilions, Güell estate 77**

1884-1926 **Temple of the Sagrada Família 76**

1885-89 **Palau Güell 78**

1889-94 **Col•legi Santa Teresa 83**

1898-1915 **Crypt Chapel, Colònia Güell 401**

1899-1900 **Casa Calvet 98**

1900-14 **Park Güell 100**

1900-02 **Casa Bellesguard 101**

1905-07 **Casa Batlló 118**

1905-11 **Casa Milà (*La Pedrera*) 119**

1909 **Parish Schools Sagrada Família 76**

died Barcelona

1858 **Josep DOMENECH i ESTAPA** — 1917

born Tarragona

1881-1904 **Model Prison 71**

1883 **Science Academy 74**

1895 **Catalana de Gas i Electritat 91**

1904 **Fabra Observatory 114**

1911 Casa Cucurella

died Cabrera de Martaró

1867 **Josep PUIG i CADAFALCH** — 1956

born Mataró

1895-96 **Casa Martí (*Els Quatre Gats*) 92**

1898-1900 **Casa Amatller 96**

1901-02 **Casa Macaya 109**

1901 Casa Muntada

1902-06 **Casa Quadras (now Museu de la Música) 112**

1903-05 **Casa Terrades (*Casa de les Punxes*) 109**

1905 **Casa Sastre 120**

1910-11 **Cassaramona Yarn Factory 128**

1923-28 **Palaus de Alfonso XIII i de Victoria Eugenia 143**

died Barcelona

1879 **Josep Maria JUJOL i GILBERT** — 1949

born Tarragona

1913–16 **Cases Torre de la Creu 404**

1914–30 **Casa Negre 405**

1918–23 **Església, Vistabella 406**

1923-24 **Casa Planells 141**

1840 1850 1860 1870 1880 1890 1900 1910 1920 1930

Introduction

by the new bourgeoisie, the captains of the textile and other industries: the clients whose values were to be celebrated in *Modernisme*.

Modernisme

In the 1870s Barcelona enjoyed an economic prosperity which allowed the development of much of the *Eixample*. The energy of *Modernisme* lasted about twenty-five years from 1880 to 1905, its achievements coming in a series of waves determined by the economic and political events of the period. The polemical use of the word *Modernisme* first occurs in the nationalist magazine *L'Avenç* ('Progress') published in Barcelona between 1881 and 1884, and later from 1889 to 1893, which sought 'an essentially Modernist literature, science and art in our land'. The movement involved all the arts. Its painters followed contemporary technical developments in Paris, interesting themselves in the transitory and ordinary as opposed to the elevated subjects of the academies. Sitges became the centre for experimental and Symbolist literature and theatre, with meetings and amateur performances held in writers' homes. Barcelona's printing houses became the focus of experiments in the design of graphics, typography and books.

In architecture, Gaudí's Casa Vicens **68**, started in 1878, and Domènech i Muntaner's Editorial Montaner i Simon **69** of 1879–86 conveniently signal the start of the *modernista* period. While their architects' careers subsequently developed in very different ways, these two buildings characterise the search for an architecture which would be both appropriately modern and which would exemplify a Catalan identity. The means for both was an eclectic historicism, but Gaudí's later usages were to include both his tectonic inventions and the entire repertoire of natural forms. In 1883 he became architect for the Temple of the Sagrada Família **76** and by 1911, when he left the Casa Milà **119** unfinished, his conventional architectural practice had stopped. Although he never established a 'school', several of his co-workers, Francesc Berenguer and Josep Maria Jujol for example, went on to have successful independent careers.

The new buildings for the University **61** had been completed in 1872 on a site suggested by Cerdà, and in that year their architect Elies Rogent was appointed the first Professor of Architecture. He taught his eclectic historical method to many of the next generation of architects, including Domènech who became the successful scholar-businessman. He taught at the University's School of Architecture and was its director in 1900 and again between 1905 and 1919, and his clients were affluent and conventional. While he himself was influenced by the

English Arts and Crafts movement, much of his work and especially his interiors could be characterised as 'Catalan Baronial'. Catalonia's crafts had not been destroyed by industrialisation and were to be encouraged in the new architecture. They included cast and wrought iron; carved and cast artificial stone; brickwork, tilework and mosaics; stained glass; stucco and *esgrafiat* work; furniture, jewellery, fabrics, posters, typography and book design. They were to be used in the service of a 'total architecture' which would 'speak' (or more often shout) of the modern world envisaged by both intellectuals and the bourgeoisie. The interiors of Domènech's Palau Ramon de Montaner **79** of 1885–93, although lacking the swirling intoxication of Gaudi's later work or the European Art Nouveau with which *Modernisme* was later and incorrectly to become identified, perfectly exemplified the programme.

In 1886, the economic boom collapsed. Preparations for the 1888 Exposició Universal were already under way, and these were pursued to camouflage the signs of economic decline. Elies Rogent was responsible for laying out the exhibition on the site of the Ciutadella fort which had been converted into a park in 1873, and he designed its main building, now demolished. The architects of *Modernisme* were represented by Domènech's Café-Restaurant **81**, Vilaseca's Arc de Triomf **82** and the two plant houses **75** by Fontserè, all of which survive. The exhibition was a success and brought the new architectural movement to the attention of its 400,000 visitors. After it closed, Domènech and Antoni Gallissà took over the Café-Restaurant and converted it to a workshop for developing the traditional arts and crafts.

In the 1890s *Modernisme* was becoming the prevailing and fashionable style in the continuing development of the *Eixample*, represented by the numerous blocks of flats by Vilaseca, Domènech and others. While the form of these blocks, of six storeys punctured by wells for light and ventilation, was largely determined by the city's by-laws, individual architects brought their particular decorative, and occasionally organisational, talents to the stereotype. Institutional buildings, however, like the Palau de Justícia **80** by Josep Domènech i Estapa and Enric Sagnier i Villavechia, continued to be executed in a variety of current European styles owing little to local innovation. The work of Josep Puig i Cadafalch, who was seventeen years younger than Domènech, stands slightly apart from that of *Modernisme* proper. Although inspired like his elders by the same romantic historicism, his work is drier, and he employed a narrower eclectic range in the extraordinarily glittering series of works of the decade 1895 to 1905, from the Casa Marti **92** to the Casa Sastre **120**.

Introduction

By 1897 *Modernisme* was fully established, and in that year was given renewed impetus as a nationalist movement with the publication of the journal *Catalonia*, and the establishment of the *Els Quatre Gats* group of artists and intellectuals who met in the café of that name in Puig's Casa Marti. Domènech's Hospital Sant Pau **106**, started in 1901, and his Palau de la Música Catalana of 1905–08 **117** are the *modernista* institutions *par excellence*. The last strictly *modernista* entry in this book, Domènech's extraordinarily vivid interiors for the Hotel España of 1905, shows that in his hands the movement was still vital. But Domènech i Estapa's Hospital Clinic **113** and Fabra Observatory of 1904 **114** employ a crude stripped Classicism, 'Mediterraneanism', which was to become the prevailing model for official buildings for the next seventy years.

Only the architecture of Josep Goday's schools suggest that the sober 'Mediterraneanism' preached earlier by Eugeni d'Ors could have benign aspects. Born in 1882, Goday worked for the municipality from 1916, and designed five of a planned programme of thirty-seven new schools between 1917 and 1923. While their plans differ widely depending on their sites, some of which are tight, others ample, all share common features. The hall is placed centrally and as far as the shape of the site would allow all the classroooms are connected directly to it with as few corridors as possible. Their architecture is 'aesthetic' rather than resolute, and its decoration occasionally weak and sentimental.

1923–30 Dictatorship, the International Exposition of 1929

Spain was neutral in the war of 1914–18, but the economy remained weak, and little noteworthy building was undertaken in Barcelona. The year 1917 was marked by social unrest and strikes in both Barcelona and the rest of Spain. The coup which established the dictatorship of Primo de Rivera in 1923 led to another building boom, and in Barcelona plans were taken up again for another international exhibition. Originally to have been held in 1917 to celebrate electricity industries, the exhibition finally opened in 1929. The plaça Espanya was monumentalised as an entrance with Jujol and Blay's baroque fountain at its centre, and leading south from this a new axis, now the avinguda de la Reina Maria Cristina, was established.

A competition for the design of the exhibition's centrepiece at the end of the axis, the Palau Nacional **149**, now the Museu d'Art Catalunya, had been held in 1917. The winning design by Pere Domènech i Roura and others is pompous, rejecting any local references in favour of a generalised Spanish Baroque. The popular exhibit, the Poble Espanyol **145**, a zoo of Spanish buildings from all regions and periods, now looks like the nadir of kitsch, and probably always did. The contributions from foreign countries included one of the most potent vehicles of international modernism, Mies van der Rohe's pavilion for the German Republic 151. This was demolished after the exhibition closed but subsequently reconstructed. The younger radical generation of Catalan architects which included José Sert and Sixt Yllescas held their own architectural exhibitions away from Montjuïc, and the group shortly afterwards established itself as GATCPAC, the Grup d'Artistes i Tecnics Catalans per al Progrés de l'Arquitectura Contemporània.

1931–36 the Republic, the Pla Macià, modern architecture

The dictatorship collapsed in 1930, and the Republic was declared simultaneously in Eibar, in San Sebastián, and in Barcelona by Lluís Companys from the balcony of the Casa de la Ciutat 14. Architects immediately became involved in plans for the city. Sert and other members of GATCPAC invited Le Corbusier to Barcelona in 1932, and he and they collaborated on a plan for the city, the Pla Macià, which was exhibited in 1934. Cerdà's legacy for once legitimised Le Corbusier's penchant for the right angle, and the new plan extended the axis of the Gran Via to the east as far as the River Besós to serve a new recreational town laid out in 'superblocks' three times the length of Cerda's, and to the west to connect Barcelona to a new deep-water port. The diagonal avenues of Meridiana and Paral·lel were extended, slicing through the Ciutat Vella to meet at the coast where their intersection was marked by three of Le Corbusier's 'Cartesian' skyscrapers.

While the Pla Macià was not implemented, modern Barcelona *has* extended to occupy the zones identified in the plan: the port has moved to the west. Sixty years later, the exemplary plan by MBMP (Martorell Bohigas Mackay Puigdomenech) for the Olympic Village, Nova Icària 212, consciously referred to the Macià plan, and placed two tall buildings at the end of an axis, the passeig Juan Carlos, extended to the coast. The contemporary monuments to the utopianism of the Republic are Sert's various housing schemes 155 and 156 and the Casa Bloc 159 of 1932–36, and the Dispensary 164 of 1934–38. There are current plans to rebuild Sert's pavilion for the 1937 Paris Exhibition, which housed Picasso's *Guernica*, on a site in the Vall d'Hebron Olympic area.

All building programmes were stopped by the Civil War which started in 1936 and finished with the collapse of Republican resistance in Barcelona in 1939. During the war most of the city's churches were attacked both on the ground and from the air, and their interiors were sacked and their roofs often burnt. Many of

Introduction

the buildings of the religious institutions were requisitioned and converted for secular social uses.

For the next thirty-five years General Franco ruled the country, and Spain almost disappears from serious architectural history, many of its leading artists either having left the country or having been killed in the war. Barcelona's only monuments to this period are the lumpy offices and banks built around and near the plaça Catalunya such as the Bank Vitalici **168** of 1942–50. In contrast to these are the early work of Coderch, the flats for ISM employees **169** of 1952–54, and various housing schemes by Martorell, Bohigas and Mackay, many of these influenced by the work of the Milanese avant-garde. Having nominated Juan Carlos heir to the vacant throne, Franco died in 1975. As new Head of State, the King steered the country towards a standard European democratic pattern, and in 1977 the first elections for over forty years were held in Spain.

Democracy and regionalisation 1977–

The years immediately following the establishment of democracy saw an extraordinary flowering of the arts in Spain, which first appeared in literature, and in the films of Almodóvar, for example. For Barcelona, the first sign of architectural revival was the programme of parks initiated by the city in the early 1980s at the suggestion of Oriol Bohigas. Echoing one of Cerdà's principles, that of even distribution, he proposed that rather than invest in one or two large 'showcase' schemes the funds for improving the city's infrastructure should be spread and spent on a larger number of smaller schemes. The city adopted the proposal and ten years later is decorated with a profusion of very intense works of small-scale architecture, a selection of which is included here. They are of variable ambition, ranging from modest and now almost invisible schemes of paving and pedestrianisation to the ambitiously avant-garde, for example Piñon and Viaplana's Plaça del Països Catalans **199** of 1981–83. Although their quality varies and some suffer from failures of design and of maintenance (the light fittings with which Catalan architects are so obsessed seem particularly vulnerable), taken together they are now one of Barcelona's unique glories.

Barcelona's bid to host the Olympic Games held in 1992 was successful, and extensive improvements to the city's infrastructure were instigated. These included the engineering works of upgrading and tunnelling much of the coastal motorway, and the construction of the outer ring road which skirts the base of Tibidabo and provides a bypass round the city for traffic between Tarragona and the north. Architects and artists were commissioned to temper the effects of these otherwise intrusive roads. The new works for the Olympics were concentrated into four areas. To the west, the area around the Campo de Futbol 171 was consolidated as a sporting centre. On Montjuïc, the old Stadium 210 was dusted off and improved, and the area to its north laid out as a promenade giving access to the Palau Sant Jordi 211, and Bofill's sullen INEFC Sports University 216. An entirely new sporting area intended eventually to serve both city-wide and local needs was constructed at Vall d'Hebron south of the Velódrom 203. At the fourth site and on the coast, the village to house Olympic athletes was built to MBMP's ambitious plan. By various architects, the flats of its new district, 'Nova Icària' 212, were designed to be sold off after the Games.

In 1986 Spain became a member of the European Community, her constitution adapted to the prevailing model of the 'Europe of regions'. Catalonia, with Barcelona as its administrative capital, became one of the fifteen 'autonomies' which now comprise Spain and achieved much of the independence and many of the institutions of a state. The buildings for these institutions are now being designed, and some, like the Palau Sant Jordi 211, have been built. Others, including the National Theatre and the Auditorium and Archive 222, at the time of writing remain projects.

The old port from Montjuïc; in the foreground, the Trasbordador Aéri

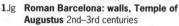

1Jg **Roman Barcelona: walls, Temple of Augustus** 2nd–3rd centuries

Plaça Nova/avinguda de la Catedral/carrer de la Tapineria etc. Temple, carrer del Paradis, 10

M Jaume I

The Romans established the colony of Barcino in the second century on a small hill rising from the coastal plain. It probably had the standard form of the Roman *castrum*, with two main streets in the form of a cross, the *cardo* running east-west on the line of carrer de Ferran, the *decumanus* north-south along what is now the carrer del Bisbe. The present plaça Sant Jaume is the site of the forum. The circuit of walls with its seventy-eight rectangular towers was built after the town was sacked by

the Franks in 263, and continued to be used in the city's defence until the thirteenth century. During the later nineteenth and early twentieth centuries a programme to remove medieval and later accretions from the walls exposed much of the lower parts of the northern and eastern sides of the circuit to either side of the Cathedral, and along carrer de la Tapineria. These are best seen at night when floodlit. The process of clearance continues still, for example at the corner of carrer Sots-tinent Navarro and carrer Sant Aulet, where parts of the *nineteenth* century city are now being removed for archaeological excavations. The four re-erected Corinthian columns of one corner of the Temple of Augustus can be seen through the arch in the gothic house at the angle in carrer del Paradis.

The medieval city 1100–1599

2Jg **Capella de Marcús** 12th century
Carrer dels Carders, 2/carrer Montcada

M Jaume I

This tiny building, named after its founder, is all that now remains of a hostel for the poor. Burnt in 1909 and 1936 and restored, the chapel's Romanesque façade and its return to carrer Montcada enclose a nineteenth-century neo-classical interior.

Detail of porch and belfry

3Je **Monastir de Sant Pau del Camp**
12th–13th centuries
Carrer de Sant Pau, 101

M Paral·lel

The monastery was founded by the Benedictine order in 977, but the visible and much-restored Romanesque work dates from rebuildings in 1127 and the following century. The sculpture of the entry façade includes Christ with Saints Peter and Paul in the tympanum, and Visigothic marble capitals to the porch. The church has a Greek-cross plan with three apses and an octagonal tower. A door in the southern transept leads to the tiny cloister, only two bays on a side, each bay separated by a massive buttress and with paired trefoil-cusped arches on capitals with carvings of animals and plants. To the west of the church is the Abbot's house of the thirteenth and fourteenth centuries.

The setting of the church to the east is being improved in the building of a community centre,

and a car park with a terraced roof (Lluís Nadal, architect, Ajuntament de Barcelona, Dte. Ciutat Vella). Next door to the church, to the west, is Goday's *Collasso i Gil* school **158**.

The medieval city

4Jb Monastir i església de Santa Anna
12th–14th centuries

Carrer de Santa Anna, 27–29

M Catalunya

Approached through an arch from the busy shopping street, the tiny church now faces its own small, quiet courtyard extended to the west by the unsatisfactory podium of the Caixa de Barcelona building. The monastery was established in the twelfth century, and the Romanesque body of the church, with its Greek-cross plan, dates from then, while the nave vault is from the fourteenth century. The church was bombed in 1936, and the stone dome over the crossing was destroyed; it was replaced with a wooden one. The chapter house, now the baptistery, and the fine two-storey cloister beyond the arch to the left of the façade, are all that

remain of the originally extensive monastery, and were built in the fifteenth century.

5Jc Església de Sant Pere de les Puelles
12th–15th centuries

Plaça de Sant Pere

M Catalunya

Rebuilt in 1147 on a Visigothic foundation of the ninth century, the church has a Romanesque Greek-cross plan with a square tower. The gothic apse and entrance portal are of the fifteenth century. The architectural details of the cloister to the south were removed to various museums in the nineteenth century. The church was burnt in 1909, and the neat and picturesque face which now faces the square is the result of a savage restoration in 1911.

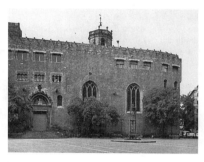

The plaça and streets to the south were pedestrianised as part of the city's parks programme.

6Jf Capella de Santa Llúcia 1257–68
Carrer de Santa Llúcia, 2/carrer del Bisbe

M Jaume I

Originally dedicated to the Mother of God and the Holy Virgins but now named after the patroness of light and knowledge, this Romanesque chapel predates the Cathedral cloister to which it now gives access. Its present rectangular barrel-vaulted interior may have lost its apse when the cloister was built. The belfry and the portal with its columns and carved capitals in the plain façade are of the same date as the rest of the building. On the corner to carrer del Bisbe is carved the length of the cana, an old Catalan measure.

7Jg **Catedral** 1298, 1317–39, façade 1887–1913
Plaça de la Seu, etc.

Ⓜ Jaume I

Work on the present Cathedral began in 1298 with the rebuilding of the earlier Romanesque structure, starting at the east end. From 1317, Jaume Fabre of Mallorca was master of works and supervised the beginning of the nave and transepts, work finished by Bernat Roca in 1388. The cloister, also supervised by Roca, was built between 1365 and 1448, and Barcelona must be awarded the distinction of having the only Gothic cloister containing both palm trees and a small flock of white geese (a reminder of those kept by the Romans on the Capitoline hill, and of the Roman greatness of Barcelona). A door in the north-west corner of the cloister leads to the Capella de Santa Llúcia **6**. The octagonal bell-towers over the transepts were added from 1389, and the Cathedral's apse was rebuilt between 1390 and 1519 when it was finally joined to the nave. The Sala Capitular (Chapter House), an impressively large single room, was built by Arnaud Bargués and finished in 1415.

The cathedral shares with Barcelona's other two great churches started in the first quarter of the fourteenth century, Santa Maria del Pi **9** and Santa Maria del Mar **11**, those characteristics of what is now recognised as 'Catalan Gothic' which distinguish it from the Gothic of northern Italy or France. (Although the Cathedral at Albi, built between 1282 and 1390 has the same single wide nave with chapels set between the buttresses.) These include the wide nave with or without aisles, its vaults restrained by external full-height solid buttresses between which chapels are set. The nave arcade is returned at the east end in a polygonal apse. The chapels are at least half the height of the nave, and restrict the amount of direct light which can be provided to the nave, this usually provided by small windows set just below the nave vault. The Cathedral is particular in having wide aisles, and the nave arcade has round arches set on columns whose clustered shafts fill out their overall octagonal shape.

In 1820, a classical façade was proposed, but the front and lantern were finally completed between 1887 and 1913 in archaeologically correct fifteenth-century Gothic style to designs by Josep Oriol Mestres and August Font.

8Jg **Carrer de Montcada** 14th century and later

Between carrer de la Princesa and passeig del Born

M Jaume I

Although visited mainly for the Picasso Museum, the carrer de Montcada is significant as the best preserved, restored and maintained medieval street in Barcelona. It grew up along the route between the mercantile and maritime sections of the medieval city, and remained a good address for nearly five hundred years until the nineteenth century when the building of the *Eixample* offered larger, more salubrious houses for the rich. Both sides are lined with the aristocrats' and merchants' small palaces or mansions, many originally of the fourteenth and fifteenth centuries. These are generally of three storeys planned round a courtyard reached by a coach-gate from the street. From the court, an external stair rises to the first floor on which the important rooms are to be found. The street façade is plain except for the occasional string course, open loggia under the overhanging roof, or little tower. Only the entry arches with their flat voussoirs, and the first floor mullioned windows with their occasional iron balconies, show any formal architectural effects. Particular houses are listed, starting at the north end from carrer de la Princesa with the lower numbers. Even numbers are on the east side, odd on the west.

12, Palau dels Marquesos de Lió, now **Museu Tèxtil i d'Indumentària**. Altered by the marques de Lió in the eighteenth century, the long irregular façade, except for its later coach door, and some of the interior spaces were again restored in 1969 to their original fourteenth-century state, when the palace was converted for use by the Cloth and Costume Museum.

14, now **Fundació Caixa de Pensions**, is a modest little one-bay house of the sixteenth century.

15, Palau Berenguer d'Aguilar, now the **Museu Picasso**, is a large five-bay house of the fifteenth century. The fine arcading to the courtyard may be by Marc Safont, master-builder of the Gothic courtyard and façade of the Palau de la Generalitat **20**.

20, Palau Dalmases, now **Omnium Cultural** originally of the fifteenth century, is a five-bay mansion with an enormous coach-door as wide as the courtyard beyond. The street façade is of the seventeenth century, when the whole palace was remodelled, and when the elaborately carved covered stair with its uneasy mixture of Catalan and baroque carving was installed. The Omnium Cultural is devoted to the promotion of Catalan culture.

25, Palau dels Cervelló, now **Galeria Maeght** has a neat symmetrical front but a slightly unruly courtyard from which a covered stair leads to the the first floor.

9Jf Església de Santa Maria del Pi 1322–1486

Plaça de Pi/plaça de Sant Josep Oriol

M Liceu

Started in the same decade as the church of Santa Maria del Mar 11, that of Santa Maria del Pi has exactly the same scheme but without either the geometrical ruthlessness or aisles of the later church. The vaults of the seven narrow bays of the 19-metre-wide nave are restrained by solid external buttresses between which are tall chapels. Above these are small windows which, with the rose window in the west wall, provide the only

illumination to the nave. The Chapter house, now the Blessed Sacrament chapel, was completed in 1486. At the south-west corner is the single very tall (54 metres) fat octagonal bell-tower added in the fifteenth century.

The special glory of the church is its setting, an irregular series of linked and now mainly pedestrianised spaces to which the church presents only partial views. To the north is the plaça del Pi with its orange trees and symbolic pine tree ('pi' is Catalan for 'pine'), and to the east and south the plaça Sant Josep Oriol.

10A Reial Monastir de Santa Maria de Pedralbes 1326–1419

Plaça del Monastir

M Palau Reial/F Reina Elisenda

The monastery was founded in 1326 by Elisende, Queen of Jaume II, and now also an eponymous Ferroviale station. Its site, well away from the medieval city, lies on the Roman via Augusta between Girona and Tarragona. Built in a single campaign over a century, and although rather sharply restored in the nineteenth century, the buildings have a coherence rare for an institution of this size, and demonstrate the full repertoire of Catalan gothic construction types. A useful modern model in the Chapter House shows the whole. The church to the west is bounded by a very large

The medieval city

three-storey cloister from which the various other functions are reached.

The plain church, its entrance marked by the octagonal bell-tower, has a single wide nave of seven bays, with side chapels. The only variations on the standard Catalan scheme are in the nave windows which are deeper than those of other contemporary examples, and at the western end which, separated from and raised above the public nave, was for the exclusive use of the monks. The tomb of the foundress is in the choir. On the north side of the cloister are the monks' dormitories, and to the south the Chapter House. The Chapel of Sant Miquel is reached from the eastern side. It contains well-preserved fourteenth-century frescoes of the Passion and the Life of the Virgin by Ferrer Bassa.

Previously housing the ceramic museum, part of the monastery is being converted to house the Thyssen collection of paintings.

11Jk **Església de Santa Maria del Mar** 1329–84
Plaça de Santa Maria/passeig del Born
Jaume Fabre (?)

M Jaume I/Barceloneta

Jaume Fabre, architect of the Cathedral, may have been the architect of Santa Maria del Mar which was designed and mostly built in a single campaign using a very simple proportioning schema of squares and half-squares for the main dimensions. This very large church, its site midway between the Cathedral and the sea, celebrates the rise of Catalonia's mercantile and maritime empire. Like most of Barcelona's churches, this one was gutted by fire in 1936 when its baroque fittings were destroyed, leaving the gothic shell starkly exposed. The single wide nave of four bays, without transepts, of the 'hall' church, the narrow aisles of the same height as the nave, and the polygonal apse are all usages typical of Catalan gothic (see Cathedral 7). The opulent ambulatory is not.

Externally, the simple engineering scheme is clearly shown in the buttresses which extend to the eaves line, and between which are incorporated chapels. Santa Maria is one of the few medieval churches in Barcelona to have a designed and completed west front, although the octagonal northern tower was finished in 1495, the southern in 1902. The fine door at the east end leads to the Passeig del Born and was designed in 1542 by Bernat Salvador.

Facing the west front of the church is the medieval **Font Gotica** of 1402. To the south, the solemn paved park of 1988, the **Fossa de les Moreres**, is a memorial to those who died defending Barcelona during the siege in 1714 by the French and Spanish under Philip V (Carme Fiol, architect, Ajuntament de Barcelona).

12Jg Església dels Sants Just i Pastor
1342–60

Plaça de Sant Just, 5-6

M Jaume I

Facing one the of city's remaining un-gentrified and traffic-choked squares, the church commemorates the tradition of Barcelona's first two Christian martyrs. Beyond the façade of 1884 is the restored medieval church: a single wide nave with chapels between the buttresses and which is terminated by a polygonal apse.

Across the square and opposite the church are the **palau Moixó** and **palau de la comtessa de Palamos**, small medieval palaces, the former refaced in the eighteenth century with rococo esgrafiats, and used by the Reial Academi des Bones Llettres; the latter is approached along carrer del Bisbe Cassador through an arch still medieval in appearance, and now houses an exhibition space, the Galeria de Catalanes Illustres, a multi-media pantheon of Catalan history.

Beyond the church to the west, the present-day carrer Ciutat is on the line of the *cardo maximus*, the central north-south street of the Roman town.

13Jg Palau Reial major and **Saló del Tinell**
1359–62

Plaça del Rei

Guillem Carbonell

M Jaume I

Restored between 1936 and 1940, the Saló is the great hall and largest part now remaining of the royal palace constructed in the reign of Pere III. Semi-circular arches with a span of 17 metres and supported on very low impost mouldings are set in diaphragm walls, and horizontal joists span between the walls. Now used for temporary exhibitions, the hall housed the many important functions of the Catalan kingdom, and was probably where Ferdinand and Isabella received Columbus on his first return from the new world in 1493. At right angles to the hall and built on an earlier foundation is the west wall and octagonal belfry of the earlier and diminutive **Capella Palatina** or **de Santa Agata** of 1319, built by Bertran Riquer as a single bare nave of three bays of arches set in diaphragm walls. From plaça Ramon Berenguer off via Laietana, the eastern flank of the chapel can be seen to be rising off the foundation of the Roman wall.

The entrance to the Saló is from the **Plaça del Rei**, one of Europe's fine and not well enough known city spaces, re-paved and pedestrianised in the 1980s. To this square the Saló presents its flank: the deep buttresses, braced by lateral vaults, which support the arched walls inside. Above and to the left are the five arcaded storeys of the **Mirador del Rei Marti**, a look-out tower of 1555–57, built at the same time as the adjoining Palau del Lloctinent **23**, and now the only remaining and late example of the type. The modern sculpture in steel at the entrance to the square is by Eduardo Chillida.

The medieval city

14Jf Casa de la Ciutat, Ajuntament de Barcelona (Town Hall) 1373, 1399–1402, 1831–47

Plaça de Sant Jaume, etc.

M Jaume I

The first date is that of the earliest extant parts of the building. The austere *neo-Grec* façade by Josep Mas i Vila which now represents the Town Hall was built between 1831 and 1847 when the plaça de Sant Jaume was also created, on the site of a church of Sant Jaume destroyed by fire in 1822. Beyond this façade is the Saló de Cent (council chamber) of 1373 with arched diaphragm walls like those of the Saló de Tinell, and to the left, to carrer de la Ciutat, the earlier artfully-irregular gothic façade of 1399–1402 by Arnau Bargués, restored at the end of the nineteenth century. The beautiful door with its large flat voussoirs gives access to the various ceremonial halls built, rebuilt and redecorated during the building's life, and to the gothic courtyard which was cut back in building the present front.

The plaça Sant Jaume is one of the most symbolic places of Barcelona and Catalonia, and it continues to be used for celebrations and demonstrations. On 14 April, 1931, Lluís Companys declared the establishment of the Spanish Republic from the balcony of the Casa de la Ciutat.

The administrative functions of the modern city are now housed in the extremely banal and unnecessarily obtrusive slab of offices behind the Casa de la Ciutat and facing plaça de Sant Miquel, the result of a competition held in 1958 (and finished in 1969, architects: Llorenç García-Bourbon and Enric Giralt i Ortet).

15Jj Drassanes (Dockyard), now **Museu Maritim** 1378–18th century

Plaça del Portal de la Pau, 1, etc.

M Drassanes

A unique survival, and tactfully restored to a plausibly primitive state, the Drassanes were begun in 1255, but the earliest work now visible—the shed to the north to carrer Portal de Santa Madrona and nearest La Rambla—dates from 1378 (Arnau Ferrer, master of works), when Catalonia's maritime empire extended as far as Athens. The building provides aisles in which ships could be built or into which they could be dragged from the sea for repair. The roof of each aisle is supported on the characteristically Catalan arched diaphragm walls used in all large-span medieval secular buildings.

The bulk of the building, including the three sheds on the corner to La Rambla, was built in the seventeenth and eighteenth centuries. This now houses the museum describing and celebrating both the imperial history and that of the fishing industry. The taller central bay in the main building was rebuilt in the eighteenth century.

On the south-western flank of the Drassanes, to avinguda del Paral·lel, are the remains of part of the seventeenth-century city walls.

16Jk **La Llotja, (Mercantile exchange)**
1380–92, 1764–94, 1802
Plaça del Palau/passeig d'Isabel II

M Barceloneta

The Llotja is primarily significant as one of the two first examples of a purpose-built exchange, together with its contemporary in Bologna, and its building marks the beginnings of banking in the mercantile city. The medieval exchange with its three-bayed aisled hall with round, not pointed, arches, was encircled by the neo-classical building by Joan Soler i Faneca in 1764–94.

17Jg **Cases dels Canonges** 14th–15th centuries
Carrer de la Pietat, 2-6/carrer del Bisbe, 4-8

M Jaume I

The Canons' houses appear to be brand-new medieval buildings, the result of their drastic restoration by Jeroni Martorell in 1927–30. The street façade of the corner building is a paradigm of that of the aristocrat's or merchant's house often used by later architects (e.g. Puig i Cadafalch) as a model for the façades of nineteenth-century merchants' houses. The flat ashlar front with its corner tower is topped by low open loggias. On to this flat field without mouldings are placed independent 'elements' with artful irregularity: important rooms have tripartite windows with incredibly slim mullions, and the door arch has very large flat voussoirs and no impost mouldings.

18Jg **Casa de la Canonja i de la Pia Almoina**
14th century
Plaça de la Seu

M Jaume I

The double name is from the time when the house was used as the residence for the Canons of the Cathedral, and from a daily ceremony instituted in 1009 of giving food to 100 of the poor. The face to the the plaça del la Seu dates from 1546 when the building was extended from the southern gable to its present northern boundary, partly over the remains of the Roman wall. The long loggia below the roof later became one of the clichés of medievalising Modernisme. The other side of the plaça is occupied by the **Casa del Degá** (the house of the Dean of the Cathedral), its façade built in 1548, restored in 1870, and again in 1919 when the architect was Josep Goday i Casals, better known for his school buildings.

19.Jf **Antic Hospital de la Santa Creu,**
now **Biblioteca de Catalunya** 1415
Carrer de l'Hospital, 56/carrer del Carme

Ⓜ Liceu

The visitor has a choice of entrances to this collection of buildings of different dates: from the north, from Carrer de l'Hospital, the later buildings are encountered first, while from carrer del Carme to the south, the earlier.

The Hospital was founded in 1401 by royal decree. A mosaic imagining the scene of the first stone-laying decorates the front of the more recent Hospital of Sant Pau 106. After continuous use over 500 years, the hospital was finally closed when the last wards were moved to the Hospital of Sant Pau in 1930. Antoni Gaudí died here in 1926 after being run over by a trolleybus.

The medieval wards were built in 1415, and are wrapped in two L-shapes round their south-facing gothic cloister of 1417 designed by Guillem Abiell. A door below the arch which connects the cloister to carrer del Carme leads to the wards with their great stone diaphragm-arches, and now occupied by a library, the Biblioteca de Catalunya. In the sixteenth century the hospital was extended in two ranges southwards from the cloister via the two external stairs, to terminate with the range along carrer de l'Hospital, which includes another chapel. The whole collection of buildings now encloses a large irregular park, a retreat from the noise and activity of the Ciutat Vella and the nearby Mercat de Sant Josep 53.

To the north of the cloister, and facing each other across a courtyard and the entrance from carrer del Carme, are the Casa de Convalescència and the Acadèmia de Medicina. The **Casa de Convalescència** was founded in 1629 when the ground floor of the two-storey arcaded courtyard was built. The upper storey of 1655–78, with its elegant Tuscan arcades, is by Josep Juli and Andreu Bosch, and the cheerful polychrome tilework lining the entrance-hall and the wall and bench of the lower arcade was added in 1680–81. The upper arcade gives access to the original convalescent wards and the chapel. The later **Acadèmia de Medicina** was built in 1762–64 by Ventura Rodriguez and Pere Virgili as the college of surgery, and contains a rooflit circular amphitheatre in which operations and dissections could be performed and viewed.

20.Jf Palau de la Generalitat de Catalunya
1418–25, 1536, 1596, etc.

Plaça de Sant Jaume/carrer del Bisbe/carrer de
San Sever

M Jaume I

The name and institution of the Generalitat origi-
nate in the thirteenth century when the name was
given to the council of the three powers of the
kingdom: ecclesiastic, military and civic. Some of
the modern ceremonial and administrative activities of the Generalitat, now the government of
Catalonia, are housed in this agglomeration of
buildings disposed round two courtyards which
now occupies a single city block. (The Parliament
of Catalonia occupies the Arsenal **31**.) The Italianate
front to plaça de Sant Jaume is the most recent
addition, built in a quiet Baroque style by Pere Blai
in 1596 and the only significant work of this date
in Barcelona. Behind this is a gothic rectangular
court reached from a gate (of 1416, by Marc
Safont) in the screen wall to carrer del Bisbe. From
this court an outdoor stair leads to the ceremonial
rooms, mostly of the fifteenth century, on the first
floor. These include the Capella de Sant Jordi built
between 1432 and 1434, also by Marc Safont. To
the north-east of the gothic court is the larger and
irregular pati del Tarongers of 1532–47, enlarged
between 1570 and 1591. The bell-tower was built
by Pere Ferrer in 1568.

The picturesque and much-photographed 'gothic'
bridge across carrer del Bisbe was built in 1928.

21.Jf Casa de l'Ardiaca i del Degà now **Institut
Municipal d'Història** 1479–1510

Carrer de Santa Llúcia, 1/plaça de la Seu/carrer
del Bisbe

M Jaume I

Facing the Capella de Santa Llúcia, the Archdea-
con's house forms a U-shape around its small
courtyard which is connected to the street by a
pedimented doorway of the Renaissance period.
The present picturesqueness of the court is enhanced by the cloister of 1870 by Josep Altamira,
and the palm tree. The marble letter-box to the
right of the door, with its carvings of a tortoise and
three birds, dates from the use of the building by
the Col·legi d'Advocats (Law Society) and is by
Domènech i Muntaner.

The medieval city

22Jg **Casa Clariana Padellàs** now **Museu d'Historia de la Ciutat** 15th and 16th centuries
Now at carrer Freneria/plaça del Rei

M Jaume I

This apparently brand-new building was translated here from its original site in carrer de Mercaders when the via Laietana was cut through the old city at the beginning of this century. It is a typical medieval merchant's house, its accommodation arranged round an open courtyard. Now a museum of the history of the city, it contains a well-arranged and interesting display of documents, drawings, artefacts, and pieces of buildings, with excavations of parts of the the Roman and Visigothic cities in the basement. From the terrace on the top floor there is an excellent view of the plaça del Rei and a panorama of many of the other monuments of medieval Barcelona.

23Jg **Palau del Lloctinent** now **Arxiu de la Corona d'Aragó** 1549–57
Carrer dels Comtes, 2/plaça del Rei
Antoni Carbonell

M Jaume I

The palace was built for the Viceroy (Lloctinent) of Barcelona as a new residence and ceremonial annexe to the medieval palau Reial **13**, and its stiffness and formality are in sharp contrast to the more cosy medieval palace. Within a rectangular plan, the rooms are arranged round two connected courts: one is large and still open, following tradition; the other of three storeys is roofed, and houses the stair. The internal architecture is mainly classical, particularly in the arcade to the open court with its Tuscan arcade, but with lingering medieval usages. Externally, the building presents very severe elevations decorated with non-Catalan window-hoods and playful turrets at the corners.

Since 1853 the building has housed the archive of the royal house of Aragón which includes four million documents dating from 448 AD.

17th and 18th centuries 1600–1799

24E **Masia Torre Rodona** now **annexe to Hotel Princesas Sofia** 1610
Carrer del Doctor Salvador Cardenal/carrer de Sabino de Arana

M Maria Cristina

Used as a reception suite by the hotel, Barcelona's earliest surviving example of the farmer's estate house or villa has been gentrified. The pyramidal composition of a central three-storey hipped-roofed pavilion flanked by two-storey wings was used for three centuries. See Introduction and **46**, **47** and **49**.

25Jj **Antic Convent de la Mercè** now **Capitania General** 1639–42, 1928
Passeig de Colom, 14-16

Santacana brothers

M Barceloneta

The classical two-storey cloister of the former convent, contemporary with that of the Casa de Convalescència **19**, is concealed by two more recent façades: to the north the earlier, connected to the church of la Mercé **39** by a bridge, and the later, to the passeig de Colom, in pretentious Tuscan of 1928, by Adolf Florensa i Ferrer and built to coincide with the exhibition of 1929. Barcelona's former monasteries and convents have had many uses: this one is now occupied by soldiers.

17th and 18th centuries

26Jf **Església de Betlem** 1681–1732
La Rambla, 107/carrer del Carme, 2
Josep Juli, project
M Liceu

The original seventeenth-century design for the Jesuits was by Juli, but the church was eventually built by Pere Tort, S.J. and Didac de Lacarse. The broken charred stones of the upper part of the façade are witnesses of the last occasion on which the church was gutted by fire, in 1936. The original fine frontispiece was not damaged, but the interior was subsequently rebuilt without its original sumptuous Baroque fittings and decoration, revealing the design's strange amalgam of Catalan Gothic and Counter-reformation ideas. The vault of the wide nave is supported on lateral buttresses which form the walls of the side chapels, and through which are cut the arches of the galleried aisles. The galleries originally carried screened 'boxes' for worshipping aristocrats, like those of the church of La Mercé **39**.

27Je **Obelisk of Santa Eulàlia** 1686
Plaça del Pedró

M Sant Antoni

Santa Eulàlia is the patroness of Barcelona, and it is this rather than any instrinsic qualities of the monument which marks the site of her crucifixion which accounts for its absurdly complicated history. The column surmounting the public fountain is by the scupltors Tremulles and Bonifaç. In 1823, attempts by the authorities to move it were prevented by popular protest. Three years later, the then Capitan General removed it to use as part of a fountain. His fountain was destroyed in 1936, and the present arrangement is by Frederic Marés, done in 1952.

On the north side of the plaça, at carrer del Carme, 106, is an eighteenth-century industrialist's house, the **Ca l'Erasme**. The ruined church on the east side is that of **Sant Llàtzer**, one of the oldest foundations in the city, now perhaps awaiting the rejuvenation of the plaça through the 'parks' programme.

28Jf **Església de Sant Sever** 1699–1705

Carrer de San Sever, 9-11/carrer del Bisbe

Jaume Arnaudies and Joan Fiter

M Jaume I

This small church was established by the clergy of the Cathedral whose cloister it faces. It has a single nave with side chapels and a polygonal apse, and the extravagant internal decorative scheme of its generic late baroque interior surprisingly survived the fires of 1936.

29E **Masia can Planes** now **Offices of Club de Futbol Barcelona** 1702

Avinguda del Papa Joan XXIII, 2-14/carrer de la Maternitat

M Palau Reial

Now isolated and the ceremonial and unlikely home of the Football Club, this former farmhouse is a smaller version of the type (see Introduction and **46**, **47** and **49**), but with all its characteristics: a central three-storey square block, a loggia on its top floor; and the two lower wings with their monopitch roofs at the sides. The only formal architecture is in the broad surround to the front door: a standard Catalan arch.

30Jb **Església de Convent dels Paüls** now **church of Sant Pere Nolasc** 1710–16

Plaça de Castella

M Universitat

Formerly belonging to a convent destroyed in 1939, and now that of the parish in which it stands, the church was never designed to be freestanding and is now largely an artefact of its various restorations. The dome with its decorations of yellow and green tile is original, its volume providing the only interest to the otherwise un-exuberant baroque of the interior.

17th and 18th centuries

31Jl **Arsenal de la Ciutadella** now **Parlament de Catalunya** and **Museu d'Art Modern** 1727–48
Parc de la Ciutadella

G. Pròsper de Werboom

Ⓜ Ciutadella

After the ramparts of the Ciutadella were finished in 1727, the fort was equipped for the military with the buildings of a self-contained town. These were arranged within the rough circle of the inner walls and on either side of the Plaça d'Armes (parade ground), and housed a garrison of 8,000 soldiers. By the beginning of this century all but three of the buildings had been demolished, and the plaça was absorbed into the gardens of the park. The oval of cypress hedges enclosing the pool was laid out in 1917 by Jean C.N.Forestier (who laid out and landscaped much of Montjuïc), and the sculpture *Desconsol* in the centre is by Josep Llimona, 1906 (see also Monument to Dr Robert **125**).

The huge sober Arsenal, its design like that of the fortifications from French military textbooks with no concessions to local taste or practice, domi-nates the eastern side of the parade ground. Abandoned when the Ciutadella was dismantled, the building was subsequently converted by Pere Falqués into a royal palace at the end of the nineteenth century when the military architecture of the central bays was ornamented with civil and un-French *esgrafiats*. The museum of modern art (modern as in *Modernisme*) has been housed in the back and sides of the Arsenal since 1902, and the Parliament of Catalunya was re-installed in the central part of the building in 1980.

Facing the Arsenal across the plaça, the **Capella de la Ciutadella** by Alejandro de Rez is the prettiest of the group, its style more French than Spanish, but with a standard Catalan or counter-reformation plan of a single nave with side-chapels. Externally, its elliptical dome is decorated with tiles, and the single cylindrical bell-tower enhances the picturesqueness of the composition. Next to the Chapel, to the north, is the small **Palau del Governador** from which the military governor ruled the city until 1869, designed in 1748 by de Werboom, influenced by French taste, complete with mansard.

32Jf **Església de Sant Agustí Nou** 1728–52
Plaça de Sant Agustí Nou
Alexandre de Rez, Pere Bertran, Pere Costa
M Liceu

Stripped-down baroque never had much success and, its original ornament destroyed by fire in 1835 and again in 1936, the interior of the convent church is now of little interest. It has a nave of five wide bays terminating in a crossing which supports an elliptical dome. The beginnings of the later façade to the as yet un-reformed square are by Pere Costa, its railings by Elies Rogent, and the return elevation to the east presents an interestingly ruined wall topped by the chapels' rooflights.

33Jb **Casa de la Caritat, cloister** now **Oficines del Centre d'Estudis i Recursos Culturals** 1743
Carrer de Montalegre, 5/carrer de Valldonzella, 13-25

M Universitat

On its corner and now one of the anchors in the current massive reconstruction of the district to which the original religious foundation gave its name, the building encloses the restored square cloister. Its pattern follows that of the Casa de Convalescència **19** of the previous century. The proportions here, however, are widened and the Tuscan order is made to carry three-centred arches supporting the doubled rhythm of the arcade above. Some of the tilework which decorates the walls and ceiling is original; the rest was restored in 1928-30. The building is now owned by the City and used as a conference centre.

17th and 18th centuries

34Jf Església de Sant Felip Neri 1748–52

Plaça de Sant Felip Neri

M Jaume I

Facing a picturesque irregular square which, complete with its fountain and two acacias, could have been one of the models for Camillo Sitte's urbanistic theories, the church is upstaged by its setting. It is a sober, academic product of the counter-reformation, an oratory as specified by St Philip and as first developed in Rome's *Gesù*: a wide three-bay nave, with screened private 'boxes' above the chapels. The elaborate altar was built later than the body of the church at the end of the eighteenth century. To the west of the church is a cloister of the original Oratorians' residence.

Next door to the church on the right, displaced when the via Laietana was built and twice relocated and reconstructed, is the Renaissance façade of the **Casa Gremial dels Calderers**, originally a house but used from the sixteenth century as the guildhall of the coppersmiths. Opposite on the other side of carrer Montjuïc is the facade of the hall of the shoemakers, the **Casa Gremial dels Sabaters** of 1565, moved from its original site near the Cathedral.

35I Castell de Montjuïc now **Museu de l'Exèrcit (Military museum)** 1751–79

Montanya de Montjuïc

M Paral·lel, then funicular

Montjuïc had been the site of a medieval watchtower, but the development of artillery made it a suitable site for a defensive fort commanding the city and the port and its approaches. The history of the castle follows that of Catalonia and the Spanish state (Lluís Companys, the President of Catalonia, was executed here in 1940). The first castle was built in 1640 during the Wars of Succession, to be rebuilt in 1694. The present rectangular fort on the crown of the hill, surrounded by its stellated ramparts straight from an engineer's textbook, was reconstructed by Martin de Cermeño, the military engineer of the contemporary Ciutadella and Barceloneta **36**, between 1751 and 1779. The present castle is the only indication of what the huge Ciutadella, demolished in the nineteenth century, must have looked like.

The climb or funicular ride to the castle is rewarded by a fine view of the whole city, best seen from the bar on the rampart's northern salient and in the afternoon when the sun is behind it.

36J La Barceloneta begun 1753

Passeig Nacional/plaça de Sant Miquel/passeig Maritim

Francesc Paredes, Juan Màrtir de Cermeño

Ⓜ Barceloneta

The establishment of the planned quarter of Barceloneta, appropriately laid out by military engineers like a barracks or colony, is the direct consequence of the battles over Catalonia in the early eighteenth century. In 1714, Philip V, the Bourbon king of Spain, laid siege to Barcelona for eleven months. After subduing the city, he ordered the construction of an enormous fort, the Ciutadella, in the Ribera district at the south-east corner of the city walls. Barceloneta was a new district for the displaced inhabitants of Ribera, its site suggested by Pròsper de Werboom, architect of the Arsenal **31**, on the sandy triangle between the port and the sea. The plan consists of a grid of very closely-spaced streets running north-south, crossed by more widely-spaced roads, now the main access to the beach beyond. The original two and three-storey houses have now largely been replaced with much taller and more oppressive tenements entirely surrounded by streets. However, the only open space planned for the district, its small plaça with its contemporary church **37**, retains something of its eighteenth-century scale.

37J Església de Sant Miquel del Port
1753–55, 1863

Plaça de la Barceloneta

Damià Ribes, Pere Màrtir de Cermeño, Francesc Paredes

Ⓜ Barceloneta

An unlikely work from Cermeño, a military engineer: the plaça has been carved out of the toy-like grid of Barceloneta to give importance to this diminutive neoclassical confection, its façade (sculptor, Pere Costa) an equally miniature paraphrase of Rome's Gesù. The plan, extended in 1863, is biaxially symmetrical: of three by five bays, each alternate bay of the nave has a shallow dome daylit by a cupola. The whole is united by a Roman Doric order, its frieze decorated with a gilded mixture of Christian and secular symbols.

Enthusiasts of Barcelona's markets should visit the covered one just north of the plaça.

17th and 18th centuries

38Jc Casa del Gremi de Velers (Guildhall)
1758–63

Via Laietana, 50/plaça del Mestre Lluís Millet

Joan Garrido

M Urquinaona

Although saved from destruction when via Laietana was built, the present coherent appearance of the silk-weavers' hall is deceptive: only the façade to Laietana is original, the other two are later pastiches. The exuberant *esgrafiat* decoration with atlantides, caryatids, putti, garlands and residual architecture cannot disguise the clumsy proportions of the storey-heights, or the weak cornice, more appropriate to a picture-frame than a building. The decoration of the southern face was done in 1931.

39Jj Església de La Mercè 1765–75

Plaça de La Mercè, 1-3

Josep Mas i Dordal; Carles Grau, sculptor

M Barceloneta

The church is devoted to the cult of Our Lady of Mercy, who appeared in Barcelona to Jaume I among others to propose the founding of an order to save Christian prisoners from North African pirates. Her feast as patroness of Barcelona is celebrated at the end of September when there are still city-wide celebrations, now mostly secular. This civic importance is reflected in the architecture of the church which, however, was not spared from burning in 1936.

The façade is of thoroughgoing, if seventeenth-century, Roman baroque, enlivened by its single more Catalonian octagonal tower and decorated with Grau's statues. The exterior of the dome was re-covered with polychromed tiles by Joan Martorell in 1888. The plan is a Roman cross with a domed crossing, and the most elaborately decorated elements of the marble-clad interior are the gilded privacy-screens to the galleries. The encrusted medieval cult-image behind the altar is of 1361.

The plaça in front of the church was re-paved, and the sculpture of Neptune installed, in 1985 (municipal architects Rosa M. Clotet, Ramon Sanabria and Pere Cassajoana, Ajuntament de Barcelona), and some of the dowdy façades round it are now being re-painted. To the right of the church and connected to it by a bridge is the back of the former Convent de la Mercè now the Capitania General **25**.

40Jf **Palau Moja** 1771–90

La Rambla, 118/carrer de la Portaferrisa, 1-3

Josep Mas i Dordal and Pau Mas i Dordal

M Liceu

This palace was, like the Palau de la Virreina **41**, among the first to be built on a site made available by the culverting of the river which runs along the line of the Ramblas, and the destruction of a part of the old city wall which followed it on the east side. The palace's more rustic architecture lacks the aristocratic assurance of the contemporary Palau de la Virreina and its ground-floor arcade is a modern alteration. The present cheerful painted decoration which largely substitutes for modelling on the façade to the Ramblas was done in the early nineteenth century; it is probable that the original decorative scheme was even more exuberant.

The ground floor has become a shop for the publications of the government of Catalonia, including books on the economy, planning, architecture and art of the region.

41Jf **Palau de la Virreina** 1772–78

La Rambla, 99

Josep Ausich, Carles Grau

M Liceu

This grand aristocratic house, and the Palau Moja **40**, and Casa March de Reus **43** on the other side of the road, were among the series of those built in the 1770s to take advantage of the spacious new sites made available when the re-ordering of the Ramblas outside the line of the old city walls was carried out by the military engineer, de Cermeño. The Palau de la Virreina was commissioned by Manuel Amat, the Viceroy (Virrei) of Peru, but he died before it was completed, and it was lived in eponymously by his widow, the Virreina.

To the Ramblas, it presents a cool façade of five bays, decorated with a giant order of pilasters, Spanish-rococo window hoods, and a full complement of vases, all by Grau, architect and sculptor. Beyond are a covered vestibule from which stairs give access to the main rooms on the first floor, and two open carriage-courts, one elliptical and one rectangular. The building now houses temporary exhibitions of art and, to the left of the entrance, an art bookshop.

17th and 18th centuries

42Jj Palau Sessa-Larrard 1772–78
Carrer Ample, 28/carrer de la Mercé, 15
*Josep Ribes i Margarit, Joan Soler i Faneca,
Carles Grau*

M Barceloneta

Carrer Ample was cut through the southern edge
of the medieval city in the middle of the sixteenth
century to connect the southern end of the Ramblas
to the area around the Llotja and the Porta del
Palau. The street immediately became attractive
to aristocrats who then built mansions along it.
Two centuries later the tradition continued, and
this largest of their palaces is an eighteenth-
century example of the type, built for the Duke of
Sessa but subsequently bought by the banker
Larrard. The influences are mainly French and
neoclassical, with very delicate modelling to the
façade by Carles Grau, who was responsible for
the very fine front door, the columns of which
support an iron balcony. The building is planned,
however, round the traditional Catalan courtyard
from which a ceremonial external stair leads to the
first floor.

43Jj Casa March de Reus 1780
La Rambla, 27-29
Joan Soler i Faneca

M Drassanes

One of the series of mansions built along the
Ramblas after the street was re-ordered (see also
Palau de la Virreina **41**, Palau Moja **40**), this house
was built for a merchant from Reus rather than for
an aristocrat. It has a regular rectangular plan with
a courtyard, and a garden at the back. The same
calm, dry taste of the Virreina prevails, but without
Grau's sculptural expertise. The modelling, here
with a giant Ionic order, can only just project itself
from the surface. The attribution to Soler i Faneca,
architect of the neoclassical casing of the Llotja **16**,
is uncertain.

(Under scaffolding at the time of writing.)

44Jj **Teatre Principal** 1790, 1847–66

La Rambla, 8

Francisco Cabrer

M Drassanes

There has been a theatre on this site, just outside the medieval walls, since 1603 when the first was established by royal charter. This was built of wood, and both it and its successors of 1728 and 1787 were, as theatres tended to be, destroyed by fire. The core of the present building of 1790 was designed by Cabrer, a military engineer, to provide the only venue in Barcelona suitable for Italian opera. After being enlarged in 1802, the convex neoclassical façade, which reflects a curve in the now vanished city wall on the opposite side of the Ramblas, was added in 1847–66 by Francesc Daniel Molina i Casamajó. Its most recent use was as rehearsal space for the Liceu. Now the Eurosex establishments which recently infested its ground floor have been banished in the attempts to make the southern end of the Ramblas less seedy, and the building is being restored and parts of it converted into a cinema.

45Jk **Duana vella (Old Customs House)** now **Palau del Govern Civil** 1790–92

Avinguda del Marqués de l'Argentera, 2/plaça del Palau

Miquel de Roncali

M Barceloneta

One of the series of large institutional buildings clustered just inside the old Portal del Mar, the main gate from the city of Barcelona to its port, the Customs building with its bulk, and the poster-sized allegorical sculpture in the panel above the entrance both serve to demonstrate the importance of maritime trade to the city. The building has a simple rectangular plan with a central courtyard. Over the century following its construction, the focus of the port's activities moved west, resting for a while at the Portal de la Pau at the southern end of the Ramblas, and in 1902 the customs moved to a new building there: the Duana Nova **94**.

46A **Masia can Raspall** now **Estudis Generals *Lluís Vives*** 18th century

Passeig de Manuel Girona, 33-35

M Palau Reial

Now hemmed in by blocks of flats but with some of its original outbuildings and open space, the former farmhouse is well maintained, and retains some architectural pretensions in its decayed *esgrafiat* decoration.

17th and 18th centuries

47C Masia can Fargas 18th century
Passeig de Maragall, 383-389/avinguda de
Frederic Rahola, 2-3

M Horta

A loggia and tower have been added to the standard masia pattern producing a picturesque jumble
of formerly rural buildings which are now contained
on a suburban plot. The farmhouse has been
gentrified into a dwelling: a 'ranch-style home'.

48C Laberint d'Horta 1791
Passeig de la Vall d'Hebrón
Domenico Bagutti

M Vall d'Hebrón

The axis on which the house and garden were
organised has been appropriated by the Velódromo
203, behind which is the entrance to the estate
which from 1971 has been a public park. The
nucleus of the estate was the medieval house at
the entrance which was Arabised in the nineteenth
century. Beyond lie the gardens laid out from 1791
for Joan Desvallas, *marquès* of Llupià and Alfarràs.
Designed by the Italian engineer Bagutti, they
constitute the most complete and well-preserved
example of a neoclassical garden-estate in Barcelona. Rising symmetrically up and into the hill via
paths, steps and terraces, they are decorated with
fountains and basins and delicate if architecturally-
dry pavilions. The design is loosely based on an
allegory of the *Stages of Love*. The most popular
feature with the public is the large square maze
(*laberint*) of trimmed cypress hedges. The wilder
parts of the garden are planted with indigenous
species, mostly various types of pine and cypress.

49D **Masia les Carasses** now **Grupo Escolar Ignasi Iglesies** 18th century
Passeig Torras i Bages, 108-128
Jaume Oliveras

M Sant Andreu/Torras i Bages

The most elaborately architectural of the masias listed, 'les Carasses' has a named architect and none of the characteristics of the earlier buildings. The farmhouse has become a classical country villa; a three-storey block with a flat cornice. The enclosed wings of tradition are replaced by open arcaded loggias.

50Jb **Palau Sabassona** now **Ateneu Barcelonés** 1796
Carrer de la Canuda, 6

M Catalunya

Originally a large and conventional neoclassical house for Josep Frances Ferrer de Llupià, baron de Sabassona, the palace has undergone many alterations, and only the façade is of the eighteenth century. From 1906, when it was converted by Josep Font i Gumà and Josep Jujol i Gilbert, the building has been occupied by the Ateneu (Atheneum), founded as a learned institute in 1836, and its huge private library. The eastern elevation was re-styled in 1968 when the plaça Villa de Madrid was enlarged.

Parc de l'Espanya Industrial 1982–85 202

51K **Cementiri de l'Est** or **Cementiri Vell (Cemetery)** 1818–19

Avinguda d'Icària

Antoni Ginesi

M Lacuna

Two large cemeteries were built in Barcelona in the nineteenth century. The later, the Cementiri Sud-oest, was built on the seaward slopes of Montjuïc, while the Cementiri de l'Est was built on flat land near the sea. The layout of both is that of a standard cemetery of Mediterranean Europe: coffins are arranged up to seven rows high between stone slabs to make walls which can be left free-standing or formed into courts. While Cementiri Sud-oest now appears to be a hill-town for the dead, here the effect is that of a neoclassical roofless library, the two courts or 'rooms' providing for different generations and classes. The neo-Etruscan ornaments may be the particular taste of Ginesi, its Italian architect, and his monumental entrance gate and pylons now form the eastern climax of the Avinguda Icària, one of the two axes around which the Olympic Village **212** of 1990–02 was organised. The cemetery was extended east-wards from Ginesi's now-decaying chapel in 1849–52 to the designs of Joan Nolla Cortés, and the second and later court contains individual mausolea, mostly gothic in style.

52Jk **Casa d'en Xifré** 1836–40

Passeig d'Isabell II, 2-14/Plaça del Palau

Josep Buixareau i Francesc Vila

M Barceloneta

Barcelona's only extant example of a regular city block in an elegant neoclassical style, these two buildings provided shops on the ground floor and housing above, with the urbanistic aim of consolidating the western side of the plaça del Palau. The block nearer the plaça has a rectangular plan with a cruciform of housing within, leaving four small courtyards. The other, to the west, is triangular, its eastern face built up to the angle of the now demolished city wall which here ran next to the sea. The cast iron which was to be used to such great architectural effect in Barcelona later in the century was introduced here. The whole is decorated with neo-Grec motifs with a marine iconography,

and is surrounded by handsome arcades, originally serving presumably elegant shops, but now the centre of Barcelona's cut-price electronics trade. (The formerly bohemian restaurant *Set Portes* at passeig Isabel II, 14 which serves good Catalan food would qualify as a notable interior, but for the bad taste of its lampshades.)

Industrialisation

53Jf Mercat de Sant Josep 1836–40
Plaça de Sant Josep, La Rambla

Josep Mas i Vila

M Liceu

The site of a former Carmelite convent closed in 1835 is now occupied by a thriving covered market, which with that of Santa Caterina 56 is one of the two remaining in the medieval city. The enclosing colonnade of 1836–40 is by Josep Mas i Vila, and the arched entrance which connects the plaça to the Rambla was added in 1870.

54Jf Gran Teatre del Liceu 1844–47
La Rambla, 61–65

Miquel Garriga i Roca

M Liceu

Opened in 1847 at the initiative of a group of military singers, the horseshoe-shaped auditorium was the second largest after La Scala, Milan. Like many theatres (see Teatre Principal 44), this one has suffered several fires, the most serious in 1861 when a complete reconstruction was required, carried out by Josep Oriol Mestres i Esplugas. The same architect designed the façade to the Ramblas in 1874, together with a distinguished group of Barcelona painters who decorated the grand retiring room and the salon behind the large windows on the first floor. Further work to the interior was done by Pere Falqués in 1874.

In a curious parallel with the recent history of London's Royal Opera House, the present manage-

ment of the Liceu have plans for a huge expansion of the back-of-house accommodation to the south which would occupy the entire block along the Ramblas. These are being resisted by conservationists and local citizens.

55Jj Plaça del Duc de Mendinaceli 1844–49
Between carrer Josep Anselm Clavé and passeig de Colom

Francesc Daniel Molina i Casamajó, and Josep Anicet Santigosa i Vestraten, sculptor

M Drassanes

On land given by the Duke of Mendinaceli, the square was laid out south of the carrer Josep Anselm Clavé, and while it now opens out to the sea, its southern end was originally bounded by the city's wall which ran along what is now the passeig de Colom. The city's first cast-iron monument of 1851 is a shaggy corinthian column on a base decorated with marine imagery including four boys riding dolphins into a pool. It is topped by the statue of the Catalan admiral Galceran Marquet who, in 1331, led the state's fleet against that of Genoa.

56Jg **Mercat de Santa Catarina** 1848

Avinguda Francesc Cambò

Josep Buixareau and Francesc Vila

M Jaume I

A crisply-designed freestanding market with residual neoclassical architecture and straightforward engineering by the architect of Casa d'en Xifré **52**, Santa Caterina is one of the several markets still serving the Ciutat Vella. Its continued existence is a reminder of the extent to which much of Barcelona retains its nineteenth-century economy and the urban structure of its neighbourhoods (*barris*). See also the markets of Sant Josep **53**, Born **64**, and Sant Antoni **67**.

57Jf **Plaça Reial and approaches** 1848–59

Plaça Reial, passeig de Madoz, passeig de Colom, passeig de Baccardi

Francesc Daniel Molina i Casamajó

M Liceu

A plaça was originally proposed here in 1822 on the site of an abandoned convent, but after various suggestions, which included a grand theatre and a galleria which would have preceded that of Milan, a competition to design a square was finally held in 1848. This was won by Molina, who was responsible for the earlier plaça del Duc de Mendinaceli of 1844 **55**, and the fountain of 1855 **58** in the plaça del Palau. Aerial photographs and one of the more popular current postcards show how sharply the square was cut like a biscuit out of the pastry of the existing city. This severance was partly mended by the two axial approaches from the north and west; and notably by the passeig de Baccardi of 1856, one of Barcelona's few authentic arcades, with its glass roof and glass bridge, between the southwest corner of the square and the Ramblas. The square's nondescript Italianate architecture does not quite match the severity of the urban gesture, and its arcades have gradually succumbed to the sleaze of the southern end of the Ramblas. It was drastically and handsomely re-paved in the 1980s by architects Frederic Correa i Ruiz, and A. Milà, leaving the existing palm trees surrealistically stranded. The two restored multi-branched lampposts in cast iron, topped by Mercury's helmet, are by Gaudí, his only public commission (there are two more in the plaça del Palau). The central fountain, also in cast iron, represents the Three Graces.

Cast iron lamp-post by Gaudí

Industrialisation

58Jk Font del Geni Català (fountain) 1855

Plaça del Palau

Francesc Daniel Molina i Casamajó, and Hermanos Baratta, Josep Anicet Santigosa i Vestraten, sculptors

M Barceloneta

The installation of this fountain marked the conclusion of the works started at the end of the eighteenth century, with the re-casing of the Llotja **16** and the building of the Customs House **45**, to constitute the plaça del Palau to the north of the main gate into the port. Much too small for its present setting, and stranded as an island in the torrent of commercial traffic on passeig Isabel II, its dedication to the Catalan genius is ironic, given Barcelona's success as one Europe's largest centres of car manufacture. The allegorical sculptural programme is of the rivers of four of Catalonia's provinces. The plaça also contains two of the four cast-iron lamp-posts by Gaudí; the others are in the plaça Reial **57**.

59F First residential building 1863

Carrer del Consell de Cent, 340/carrer Roger de Llúria, 49

Ildefons Cerdà i Sunyer

M Passeig de Gràcia

The principles and history of Cerdà's plan of 1859 for the Eixample are described in the Introduction, pages 11–13. This building is the first demonstration of his intentions towards its built form. Its corner site, facing one of the small squares created by the cut-off corners of the blocks, avoids questions about the subsequent development of the block, and although the building's form is unremarkable this was one of the propositions of the plan. It has commercial uses on the ground floor and four floors of residential space arranged as flats above, its total height falling within the plan's specification of 20 metres minimum and 24 maximum. Although Cerdà trained as an architect, his work here is either inept or innocent. The otherwise completely flat façades are relieved only by diffident string-courses, which suggest that none of the storeys is of the same height, and by the balustrades to the deeply-recessed windows. The decorative painting scheme is by Beltramini, and was restored in 1986.

60F Passatge Permanyer 1864

south of carrer de Consell de Cent between carrer de Pau Claris and carrer Roger de Llúria,
Jeroni Granell i Barrera

M Passeig de Gràcia

That the 'island' or 'perimeter' block had no place in Cerdà's plan was confirmed shortly after that plan was approved by the building of this little street of two-storey houses in Italianate-Arabic style, set back behind their fenced front gardens: the whole effect is very English. The street is gated and gentrified and the houses have become the consulting rooms of orthodontists and gynaecologists. See also the **passatge Méndez Vigo** in the next block, to the north, off carrer de Consell de Cent, where a once-similar street has become overwhelmed by later development.

61F Universitat de Barcelona 1868–72

Plaça de la Universitat
Elies Rogent i Amat

M Universitat

A university was first established in Barcelona in 1300, but the institution has not had a continuous history. The present one's origins are in the constitutionalist period of the 1820s, and it was eventually refounded in 1847 as an autonomous body. In 1958 all but the ceremonial and some administrative functions of the University were moved from the present site to a new one at the north-western end of the avinguda Diagonal. Cerdà's plan made no general proposals for the location of particular or important buildings within it, although the two hospitals were placed on the outskirts and at opposite ends of the *Eixample*. However Rogent as architect was able to discuss and agree with the urbanist the site for the new University: the amalgamation of two standard blocks facing the irregular *rond-point* formed by the intersection of two of the *rondas* which trim the Ciutat Vella, and with a frontage to one of the wide streets proposed in the plan, the Gran Via des les Corts Catalanes.

Rogent, born in 1821, had travelled widely in Europe, and he designed the University building in the latest European style for a new institution. Its plan is neoclassical, perhaps deriving directly from Durand. A central block contains the grand vaulted entrance hall and upstairs the ceremonial hall and library, while the teaching accommodation is arranged around two courtyards behind the flanks of

the main elevation to the Gran Via. The style is mixed, but derived mainly from German late romanticism, and *rundbogenstil* which also has appropriate resonances of Catalan romanesque. The two delicately arcaded courtyards are particularly fine, and the garden in the open yard at the back of the building is an arboretum dating from 1932.

When the building was completed in 1872, Rogent, aged 51, was appointed head of the newly-formed School of Architecture where the Faculty subsequently taught his programme of academic eclecticism to many of those who were to become the architects of Catalan *Modernisme*, and who in their turn became professors at the School.

Industrialisation

62F Universitat Industrial 1870–05

Carrer del Comte d'Urgell, 187/carrer de Rosselló

Rafael Guastavino i Moreno, Joan Rubió i Bellvé

M Hospital Clínic

The Industrial University now occupies four of the standard blocks of Cerdà's plan. The earlier Engineering school had occupied the buildings of the old Battló factory of which the huge chimney of 1868 remains. The University proper was constituted between 1914 and 1925 and many of its buildings by Joan Rubió i Bellvé, one of Gaudí's assistants, date from 1927–31. These include the extraordinary chapel, its diaphragm walls pierced by parabolic arches. Since extended, the whole University now forms a residential campus of very plain brick warehouses.

63JI Parc de la Ciutadella 1873

Passeig de Picasso, passeig de Pujades, carrer de Wellington, passeig de Circumval·lació

Josep Fontserè i Mestres

M Ciutadella/Arc de Triomf

Pool and hedges, Jean C.N. Forestier, 1917

The huge Ciutadella at the south-east corner of the city walls was started in 1727, and its main buildings finished by 1748 (see the Arsenal **31**). It remained the headquarters of the military governor of Barcelona until 1869, ten years after Cerdà's plan for the *Eixample* was approved. In that year the Catalan General Prim decreed the transfer of the fort to the city. Fontserè won the competition held in 1873 for the design of a public park and housing to replace the fort. The park was the only one then serving Barcelona, and it still is the largest after Montjuïc. Some of Fontserè's plan and landscaping survived the staging of the International Exhibition of 1888 (see the Hivernacle and Umbracle **75** and Café-Restaurant **81**). The large cascade and fountain **66**, and the boating-lake in the north-east corner were built in 1875–81, and much of the south-east corner is now enclosed for the Zoo. In 1990, traffic was excluded from the park's central north-south road, and this axis was consolidated to the north with two new rows of palm trees which extend via the passeig Lluís Companys as far as the Arc de Triomf **82**.

Tàpies's *Homage to Picasso*

The wide pavement alongside the western boundary of the park, the **Passeig de Picasso**, was reformed in 1988 with new planting and a small canal (architects: Rosèr Amado and Lluís Domènech), and Tàpies's glass-enclosed sculpture *Homage to Picasso* at its centre.

64Jg **Mercat del Born** 1873–76

Carrer del Comerç, 29

Antoni Rovira i Trias, city architect and Josep
Fontserè i Mestres, Josep M. Cornet i Mas

M Barceloneta/Jaume I

One of the many new buildings for specific uses
built during the early years of the implementation
of the Cerdà plan, and a thoroughgoing engineer's
building, Barcelona's very large central market
was designed and built quickly, exploiting the
properties of iron and steel and other dry, prefabricated materials. The rectangular plan has a wide
central aisle marked at either end by a gable and
flanked by two subsidiary aisles which have hipped
roofs at the corners. An aisle the same width as the
first is arranged on the central cross-axis, and the
crossing of the two is marked by a shallow octagonal lantern crowned with a little cupola which
provides the building's only 'architectural' decoration. In 1985 the market was converted for use as
an exhibition and performance space, and the
structure, the fine tilework and louvres which make
up most of the exterior walls, and the polychromed
tiled roof were restored.

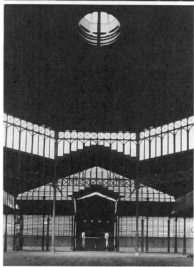

65Jh **Diposit d'aigua del Parc de la Ciutadella**
(Reservoir building) 1874–80

Carrer Wellington, 50

Josep Fontserè i Mestres, Josep M. Cornet i
Mas

M Ciutadella/ Arc de Triomf

A magnificent work of engineering from the team
that designed the contemporary Mercat del Born
64. The building's function was to hold on its roof
an enormous square tank of water supplying the
fountain and lake of the Parc de la Ciutadella. This
tank is supported on thick parallel brick walls
pierced by arches and with barrel-vaults between
them, the whole buttressed round the perimeter.
Square towers at the corners complete the architectural composition and give access to the roof.
The building, now cleared of its machinery and
its brickwork cleaned, is used as an exhibition
space. (Conversion by Ignacio Paricio, Lluís Clotet
and Joan Sabater, 1988.) A temporary bridge from
the first-floor conveniently crosses the carrer Wellington and continues into the park, providing the
only access to and from the park's eastern side.

Industrialisation

66Jh Cascade and lake 1875–81
Parc de la Ciutadella
Josep Fontserè i Mestres

M Arc de Triomf

Fontserè inclined towards what was regarded as the English landscape style, and he designed the sinuous paths of the park which contrast with the formality of the avinguda dels Tells. The ornamental lake is picturesquely kidney-shaped, but the cascade which serves it is in an academic style derived from French models. It is monumentally placed in the corner of the park and its back faces the southern end of the Avinguda de la Meridiana which lies at forty-five degrees to the Cerdà grid. Various sculptors, including the young Gaudí, were employed for the statuary, and while his signature has not been found on them the dragons at the front of the cascade and the design of its rocks are attrib-

uted to him. He may also have collaborated in the design of the park's cast iron railings. Both cascade and lake were served by the Reservoir building 65, and from the right-hand side of the fountain a footpath and bridge lead to the building when it is open.

67Ja Mercat Sant Antoni 1876–82
Carrer del Comte d'Urgell, 1/carrer Tamarit

Antoni Rovira i Trias, city architect; Josep M. Cornet i Mas

M Sant Antoni

One of the special buildings incorporated easily into Cerdà's grid, the market occupies one whole block, and is one of the few to make good use of the block's cut-off corners. The original rational and geometrical plan had the two main market halls set on the diagonals of the block and entered at its corners. Between the arms of the halls and

next to the street there were fenced and gated service yards for the delivery of goods. At the centre where the halls cross is an octagonal lantern and ventilator. The clarity of this plan has now been obscured by the later filling-out of the block with the addition of the aisles and stalls which occupy the perimeter where the yards used to be. Like the structure of the earlier Born market 64, that of Sant Antoni is of the most refined ironwork, but this is then decorated in a more conventional Italianate style with arched panels of louvres, handsome arches with windows in the gables, and a roof patterned in orange and green tiles. (See other nineteenth century markets 53, 56, 90).

Modernisme 1878–1910

68F Casa Vicens 1878, 1883–85
Carrer de les Carolines, 24
Antoni Gaudí i Cornet

M Lesseps/Fontana

What we now see is *not* what Gaudí built. In 1925
the house was doubled in size by a new owner, with
an extension to the north-east. The extension was
designed by Serra Martinez but with Gaudí's approval. Vicens, the original client and a manufacturer of ceramic tiles, commissioned the house
from the young Gaudí in 1878. Having profited
from the short business boom which Barcelona
experienced between 1878 and 1882, he started
building in 1883, when Gaudí was already occupied in work on the church of Sagrada Família **76**.

The plan of the house appears to owe nothing to
tradition. On each floor, two rows of three intercon-
necting rooms are slid past each other, and the
shear line is marked on the façade to the street by
the corbelled projecting chimneys which culminate
in turrets. The main rooms face the garden to the
south-west, and the central room on the first floor
originally had a small shuttered outdoor room, now
filled in. The style of Gaudí's first house demonstrates neither his later use of organic, vegetable
forms, nor similar results to those which his contemporaries were obtaining from the emerging
methods of *Modernisme*. It is, however, a product
of the same eclectic methods but the sources are
almost entirely from the sharp-angled geometry
and the forms and colours of *mudéjar* architecture.
This is displayed in the brickwork bands which
separate the panels of rubble, in the corbelled and
cusp-arched window heads and particularly in the
projecting screen of triangular-arched bays to the
second floor which provides a layer of space
between the outer skin of the building and the

windows behind. (This latter reappears in the first
floor of the Palau Güell **78**.) Finally, the more
important features of the façade are enriched with
patches of chequerboard and floral tiling: the tile
manufacturer has been provided with the romance
of a vanished Spain and some of the glamour of
north Africa.

The beautiful cast-iron street railing, with its sinuous organic fan-palm forms firmly held in a square
grid, is unprecedented: it is the first indication in
European architecture of what was to flower into
Art Nouveau. When the house was extended, the
rest of the railing was moved to the entrance of the
Park Güell **100**.

Modernisme

69F Editorial Montaner i Simon now Fundació Antoni Tàpies 1879–86

Carrer d'Arragó, 255

Lluís Domènech i Montaner

M Passeig de Gràcia

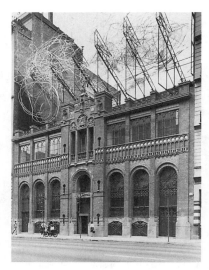

The first residential building in the *Eixample* **59** was designed by Cerdà in 1863. The Editorial was the first industrial building to survive where the architecture of the academy was employed to represent industry within the new city. In 1878 the young Domènech wrote an article 'In search of a national architecture' in *La Renaixença*, and in the following year the printing works and offices of the newspaper publishers Montaner and Simon offered the first opportunity to demonstrate the consequences of his programme. In doing so he launched what was immediately recognised as *Modernisme*. The building is rationally-planned: towards the back of the site are the sheds on two floors which originally housed the printing machinery and which have a structure in cast iron, while the two floors of editorial offices with rooms for typesetting over them face the street. The façade is a complex composition, its restlessness the result of Domènech's ambitious cultural programme which aimed to wrest from architectural history an architecture which was both appropriately modern and which would exemplify the Catalan identity.

The elements which represent the structure, the piers and round-headed arches without impost-mouldings, are in 'nationalistic' brick, rather than stone. The arches are topped by an elaborately fretted cornice above which the typesetting floors with their flat overhanging eaves ride like a tall loggia, perhaps a reminder of those of urban medieval palaces or rural *masias*. These regular bays are interrupted by the projecting full-height panel containing the front door, its top fretted and battlemented. The ornamental programme is derived from *mudéjar* brickwork, vernacular and medieval Catalan usage, and mechanistic elements like the interlocking cogs which span the central top floor windows.

In 1989 the building was converted by Rosèr Amado and Lluís Domènech for the *Fundació* for the exhibition and study of the work of Tàpies, the Catalan painter and sculptor. His wild sculpture *Núvol i Cadira* ('Cloud and chair') on the roof, is best seen at night when it is floodlit.

70Jf Passatge del Crèdit 1879

Carrer de Ferran to baixada de Sant Miquel

Magi Rius i Mulet

M Liceu/Jaume I

Not roofed, and therefore not strictly an arcade, the *passatge* otherwise demonstrates the characteristics of the type with a narrow pedestrian way connecting two commercial streets originally lined with small shops (now no longer used). The elegant frame of its structure in the then recently fashionable cast iron is shown off in the plain trabeation of the lower floors, but the upper storeys in masonry are in a very neat if mannered neoclassical style, surprising at this late date.

71E Presó Model (Model Prison) 1881–1904

Carrer d'Entença, 155

Josep Domènech i Estapà

M Entença

Another of the particular institutions to be placed within the generality of the grid of the *Eixample*, the prison occupies two blocks on its western side that were originally on the edge of the city, but are now incorporated within it. In the middle of the site the wings of the cell-blocks are arranged in a six-pointed star radiating from a central hall, one version of the ideal 'panopticon' plan evolved in England by Jeremy Bentham. The plain buildings for administration and service which occupy the

frontages to carrer d'Entença and carrer de Llaçnà Nicaragua suggest incarceration through their use of the imagery of castles. Though Domènech i Estapà was never in the vanguard of *Modernisme*, he did become Barcelona's foremost institutional architect (see also the Acadèmia de Ciències **74**, Palau de Justícia **80**, Catalana de Gas i Electricitat **91**, and Hospital Clínic **113**).

72Jj Monument to Cristobal Colom (Christopher Columbus) 1882–86

Plaça del Portal de la Pau

Gaietà Buigas i Monravà

M Drassanes

Built in time for the Exposició Universal of 1888 and anticipating the quatercentenary of Columbus's first expedition to the New World, the siting of this cast-iron column at the southern end of the Ramblas also records the drift of the city's port activity towards the west. The first gate to the port was at plaça del Palau to the east, the next here at Portal de la Pau, and the modern port is now on the other side of Montjuïc. Buigas won the competition for the design of the monument in 1882, and his cast-iron column, on its stone and fountained base 60 metres high in all, is in the grand tradition of such monuments which started with that of the Bastille in Paris in 1830, and continued with the Siegessaüle in Berlin of 1873. There is a lift to the gallery in the 'crown' at the top of the column from which views of the port, the Ramblas and the medieval city are to be had with less vertigo than those from the Transpordador Aéri across the harbour.

73F Església de Saint Francesc de Sales (Church of the Salesians) 1882–85

Passeig de Sant Joan, 88-92/carrer de València, 370

Joan Martorell i Montells

M Verdaguer

The church, school and convent for the teaching order occupy the whole of the northern half of the block. The church is in a tough, eclectic and idiosyncratic gothic, in brick rather than stone, the style owing little to the emerging *Modernisme* except in the polychrome tilework of the belfry. Martorell uses pointed arches towards the street and in the nave, but diagonal 'arches' to the transepts and lantern over the crossing, these repeated in the walls of the single-storey presbyteries to the passeig de Sant Joan.

Modernisme

74Jb Acadèmia de Ciències (Science Academy)
1883
Las Ramblas, 115
Josep Domènech i Estapà
M Catalunya

Domènech i Estapà's second building for an institution, the Academy (the first was the Presó Model **71**) presents four storeys, an octagon and two towers to the Ramblas. The flat façade is punctuated with historicist encrustations of even depth, and the third floor is decorated with low-relief terracotta panels. Like the rest of his *oeuvre*, this building cannot transcend the historicism of his method, nor achieve the *Modernisme* of architects such as Domènech i Muntaner or Puig i Cadafalch.

75Jh L'hivernacle and Umbracle (Plant houses)
1883–88
Parc de la Ciutadella
Josep Amargós i Samaranch, Josep Fontserè i Mestres
M Arc de Triomf

Part of the programme of equipping the Parc de la Ciutadella with the apparatus of a nineteenth-century city park, and lined up along the passeig de Picasso, these buildings are arranged to the north and south of the disused **Museu Martorell de Geologia**, also by Fontserè. Amargós's hivernacle to the north protects the plants from the winter cold, and consists of a pair of delicate and transparent greenhouses in cast iron with a roofed open space between them.

above: l'hivernacle; below: Umbracle

The umbracle by Fontserè provides shade but allows ventilation through its horizontal timber louvres arranged in a bulbous section. These are capped at the ends by a conventional architecture of three brick arches topped with chunks of battlement. Both buildings were appropriated for use as pavilions for the 1888 exposition, but have subsequently been restored for their original inhabitants.

76G Temple expiatori de la Sagrada Família
1883–1926 and work continues

Carrer de la Marina, 251-253

Antoni Gaudí i Cornet

M Sagrada Família

The temple has its origins in one of the popular cults which nineteenth-century lay Catholicism frequently produced. A branch of the Association of Saint Joseph, founded in Dijon, was set up in 1866 by Josep Bocabella, a Barcelona bookseller who subsequently launched the idea of an 'expiatory temple' to be built by public subscription. By 1881 subscriptions enabled the association to buy a site in a poor district of Barcelona within, but on the edge of the *Eixample*, and to commission an architect, Francesc de Pau del Villar i Lozano. The foundation stone of his conventionally-gothic crypt was laid in 1882, but Villar resigned the following year and the young Gaudí was appointed, then aged 31. He spent the rest of his life working on the building, and from 1911 when he left Casa Mila **119** unfinished, he worked on nothing else until his death in 1926.

In 1892, with the crypt completed and the walls of the apse at their present height, the work was taken over from the association by the church, and the building became an official and civic enterprise. Work was begun on the façade of the eastern transept, and its three portals were finished in 1901. The **Parochial School**, the delicate single-storey building, its wavy roof now hidden in the

building yard on the south-west corner of the site, was finished in 1909. After Gaudí's death in 1926, building continued and was supervised by his pupils and collaborators led by Domènech Sugrañes. Work stopped in 1935, and during the Civil War the building was attacked, like most of the other churches and religious foundations in Barcelona, and parts of it burnt. The site office with its Gaudí archive, models and working drawings was destroyed: a few charred remains are exhibited in the crypt, now a museum.

Gaudí worked empirically, his designs always fluid, but the general plan of the temple is conventional and evident from the various models and drawings housed in the crypt and west porch: a nave flanked by pairs of aisles meets two aisled transepts at a crossing which was to be marked with an enormous tower, lantern and look-out 170 metres high. Beyond the crossing is a raised polygonal apse. The finished building could have housed a congregation of 13,000. There was an elaborate iconographical programme to accompany the architectural elements: groups of towers stood for apostles, the number of columns in the nave for the disciples, and so on. The whole building was to be surrounded by a moat and an ambulatory on the perimeter of the site (part of this has been built at the north-east corner).

There are two sources of the building's extraordinary power and of its success as a cult-object with an international public. The first is in Gaudí's single-minded attempt to invent a rational alternative in the structural use of load-bearing masonry to pointed-arched and buttressed gothic. His informing idea was to use the parabolic arch (approximating to the inverted curve adopted by a heavy hung chain held at its ends), in which the lateral forces are transmitted within the sloping supports without the need for buttresses (an *anti*-Catalan-gothic device). These angled piers and columns are quite shocking for any observer used to the orthogonality of most monumental architecture. The second shock is in the extraordinary fecundity of his decorative imagination. Gaudí ransacked the physical world, both organic and inorganic, for programmes and motifs. This acquisitiveness was sometimes literal: much of the sculpture for the porch of the Nativity was done from studio photographs of models or, in the notorious example of the donkey, from plaster casts. Other decoration is abstracted from natural forms, while some is abstract, for example the geometrical forms of the

finials to the transept's towers. Much of the exterior and all the interior was intended to be coloured, and Gaudí with one of his assistants Josep Maria Jujol i Gilbert worked out a complete and symbolic programme: the southern aisle of the nave was to be gold and white for joy, the northern black and purple for mourning. Too rich for subsequent taste, this scheme is now restricted to the lettering on the towers and to their finials.

Since 1926, work on the building has continued sporadically, and the west porch with sculptures of the Passion by the Catalan sculptor Xavier Subirachs was the most recently finished (1952). The leaning columns of the nave now have priority, but building these in reinforced concrete cased in thin stone cut by computer-controlled machines finally sabotages Gaudí's quest for rationality in load-bearing masonry, and fatally deprives his forms of their original meaning.

77A Gatehouse and pavilions, Güell estate
1884–88

Avinguda de Pedralbes, 77/passeig de Manuel Girona

Antoni Gaudí i Cornet

M Palau Reial

Like Gaudí's other patrons Battló, and Milá, Eusebio Güell was the inheritor and captain of part of the Catalan textile industry. In 1878 he had seen Gaudí's exhibition display in Paris for the glove manufacturer Comella, and these pavilions are Gaudí's first work for him. They marked the entrance to one of Güell's country estates: on the left is the little octagonal domed gatehouse and on the right the stables and riding school. The stable is roofed with Catalan vaults supported on parabolic arches whose bays form the horses' stalls, and at the far end the square riding school has a dome lit by a lantern. The ensemble suggests a catalogue of masonry techniques: pink and yellow bricks laid in regular courses, or in open-work or corbelled; rendering and rubble. It is decorated mainly with *modernista* Moorish motifs, but with particular flourishes unique to Gaudí. The most extraordinary of these is the 5-metre wide 'dragon' gate in iron mesh and cast, and wrought, iron, a masterwork of the artisanal skill then available in Barcelona and which Gaudí could command. The iconography of the dragon is either connected with Saint George, patron of Catalonia, or it is part of a larger theme in which the estate becomes the Gardens of the Hesperides. The stables have been converted and now house the Gaudí Foundation, an archive and study-centre attached to the University.

78Jf Palau Güell, now **Museu de les Arts de l'Espectacle (Theatre Museum)** 1885–89
Carrer Nou de la Rambla, 3–5
Antoni Gaudí i Cornet

M Liceu/Drassanes

Unlike the plan of Gaudí's first house, the Casa Vicens **68**, that of this enormous town-house for Eusebio Güell is traditionally organised round a central salon. This 'patio', however, rather than being entered from the street and providing views of and access to the important rooms, is introspectively embedded in the accommodation and starts at first floor level. Nor is it open to the sky, but is covered with a perforated dome of parabolic section which rises through the remaining floors to emerge on to the roof. Here it joins the sculptured chimneys used by Gaudí in this house for the first time. Facing the street are two large doors set in parabolic arches. One is for horses, who having entered can continue via a ramp down to their quarters in the basement, the other is for people who ascend by two distinct flights of stairs and after negotiating two right-angles arrive at the first floor. At this level the *en-suite* rooms for formal occasions face the street from which they are screened by a parabolic arcade and the continuous cantilevered loggia, while the more intimate rooms are placed beyond the domed salon and facing the garden at the back. Another flight of stairs rises out of the salon and gives access to the two floors of bedrooms above. These are reached from a screened gallery which gives partial views down into the salon and up into the dome.

Although massive, and with its sumptuous and robust finishes of stone and marble, many of the details have the air of experiment or improvisation: see for example the unsatisfactory junction between the window arch to the right of the door in the salon's north wall and the support to the pendentive of the dome over it. While some Moorish usages remain, in for example the timber screens to the salon's gallery, Gaudí's work here was much closer to the 'baronial' architecture which any of Güell's contemporary industrialists in Europe would have expected. Instead of standard pointed arches, however, Gaudí provided his 'nationalistic' Catalan variant, the parabolic.

79F Palau Ramon de Montaner 1885–93

Carrer Mallorca, 278/carrer Roger de Llúria

Lluís Domènech i Muntaner (Josep Domènech i Estapà)

M Girona

The proprietors of the Editorial Montaner i Simon **69** originally commissioned Josep Domènech i Estapa to design a pair of houses on one edge of a typical *Eixample* block. The house for Simon was built by Estapa but has since been demolished. The other, for Montaner, was started by Estapa but finished by Domènech i Muntaner. It is a small freestanding 'palace' on a corner, its form remarkably severe. The influences are largely German with no trace of the delirious medievalism of the Exposició Universal. Domènech i Muntaner finished the interior and supervised its decoration including that of the central staircase. The fine polychromed sculptured mosaic panels on the exterior are by Eusebi Arnau and Becchini.

80Jh Palau de Justícia (Law Courts) 1887–1911

Passeig de Lluís Companys, 16

Josep Domènech i Estapà, Enric Sagnier i Villavechia

M Arc de Triomf

While the period of its construction coincides with that of the development of *Modernisme*, this huge (200 metres long) building owes little to that movement. Even its material, grey stone from Montjuïc, is in distinction to the favourite brick of *Modernisme*. Its plan, due largely to Sagnier, is resolutely beaux-arts, and its style a crushing Classicism with most of the architectural effort concentrated in the profile of the roof. The two wings planned round courtyards are marked with towers at the corners, while a central tower is set back behind the central entrance. It is fortunate that Justice no longer needs to present herself with such overpowering symbolism.

81Jh **Café-Restaurant** now **Museu de Zoologia**
1887–88

Parc de la Ciutadella

Lluís Domènech i Montaner

M Arc de Triomf

This is the most significant and influential of the
extant buildings constructed in the Parc de la
Ciutadella for the Exposició Universal of 1888, and
with the Editorial Montaner i Simon **69** it is one of the
masterpieces of Domènech's early career. Its
profile and plan are that of a castle in brick. Double
walls run between the square corner towers, and
a *porte-cochère* extends out from the tower on the
north-west corner to mark the entrance. The south-
east tower is extended with an octagonal drum
crowned with a spiky crow's nest with a lantern lit
by blue glass.

The Café was designed and built very quickly, and
this may account for its comparative lack of decoration. Like the Arc de Triomf **82**, it is built of
'nationalistic' brick and much of the means of
construction is left unadorned: note the exposed
steel lintels over the ground floor windows. Its
present use as a museum has allowed the large
internal spaces to remain uninterrupted.

After the Exposició closed, Domènech, together
with Antoni Gallissà, took over the building and to
further the *modernista* programme set up a workshop for the design and production of glazed
ceramics, wood carving and metalwork.

82Jd **Arc de Triomf** 1888

Passeig de Lluís Companys

Josep Vilaseca i Casanovas

M Arc de Triomf

One of the few buildings lying on one of Barcelona's
few formal axes (the passeig de Sant Joan), this
arch marked the entrance to the south of the
Exposició Universal of 1888, which was held in the
newly arranged Parc de la Ciutadella. Its position
on this axis has recently been enhanced by its
restoration and by the re-ordering of the Passeig
Lluís Companys. The design takes the form of the
Roman arch, but re-interprets it in orange and
yellow brick, and seriously disrupts the Classical
profile with the corbelled cornice. Replacing the
conventional heroic figures, the spiky crowns which
top the piers disturbingly suggest that the building
may just have suffered a mild electric shock.
Mudéjar decoration appears on the walls of the
spandrels and the returns of the arch, and further
decoration is supplied in the sculptured panels
under the cornice and in the gilded and enamelled
low-slung impost moulding.

Modernisme

83A Col·legi Santa Teresa (Convent and school)
1889–94

Carrer de Ganduxer, 85-105/carrer de Alicante

Antoni Gaudí i Cornet

F Bonanova

Gaudí received this commission while the Palau Güell **78** was being finished, and its simplicity and cheapness are in sharp contrast with the opulence of that work. Its type is similar to that of a modern office building: within the plan of 18 metres by 60 metres each of the four floors is planned with rooms on either side of a central corridor. The section, however, is elaborately articulated: central light wells punctuate the upper three floors, and light the circulation spaces which divide to run on either side of them. On the first and second floors the corridor becomes a paraphrase of a cloister, and the loadbearing cross-walls are reduced to remarkably thin diaphragms pierced by parabolic arches. These are virtuoso displays of Gaudí's traditional and innovative usages in masonry construction, as are the brick columns on the ground floor, their courses twisted against one other to produce spiral 'flutes'.

The plainness of the repetitive exterior is relieved both by the panels of rubble between the brick frames and by the triangular gables of the window hoods of the cells on the top floor which give the building its characteristic spiky roofline. The projecting porch is decorated with a coat of arms, and the wrought-iron door grille decorated with the letters S and T is particularly fine.

84Jc Cases Pons i Pascual 1890–91

Passeig de Gràcia, 2-4/ronda de Sant Pere, 1

Enric Sagnier i Villavechia

M Catalunya

Although drastically converted to air-conditioned offices in 1984, these two adjoining houses commissioned by two clients at the same time from the prolific architect, Sagnier, retain their overall form (they are contemporary with his work on the Palau de Justícia **80**). On this irregular site each house is planned round a central patio, and two towers, one round and one octagonal, are used to negotiate the exterior corners. Between these towers run the flat façades which are capped at roof level by sharp overhanging eaves, like those of the medieval palaces of carrer de Montcada. The detailing of windows and balconies is gothic whose strength has been diluted by the modern aluminium unsubdivided window frames.

85Jf **Casa Bruno Quadros** 1891–96

Rambla de Sant Josep, 82/plaça de la Boqueria

Josep Vilaseca i Casanovas

M Liceu

By the oldest of the *modernista* architects, this block of flats with its Egyptian motifs has been overlaid by the oriental dragon and sunshade decorations of the umbrella shop which used to occupy the ground floor. The effect is queasy; the cultural influences of the Exposició Universal of 1888 were not always benign.

86F **Casa Enric Battló i Battló** now **Comtes de Barcelona Hotel** 1891–96

Passeig de Gràcia, 75/carrer de Mallorca, 275

Josep Vilaseca i Casanovas

M Passeig de Gràcia

The site was a difficult one: half the width of a block facing carrer de Mallorca and a return on one of the diagonal corners to the passeig de Gràcia. The composition of the façades is a fluent exercise to produce a base of two storeys, a middle of three, and a top. These are carefully articulated in different materials, stone for the base and brick above, and their junctions are reinforced by the continuous iron balconies. The bright mosaic panels between the top floor windows are by Jaume Pujol i Bausis, *fils*. The corner above the hotel entrance has been altered; there were originally bay windows on every floor. Just along carrer de Mallorca to the west are Vilaseca's flats for Angel Battló **87**.

Modernisme

87F Cases Angel Battló 1891–96

Carrer de Mallorca, 253-257

Josep Vilaseca i Casanovas

M Passeig de Gràcia

This unified development of three blocks of flats is one of the Battló brothers' three commissions from Vilaseca. (Next door to the east is the Casa Enric Battló i Battló **86**.) Each block is divided into two bays topped by a boldly projecting gothic hood, suggesting an arrangement of vertical houses of two window bays each. This is, however, contradicted on the ground floor by the central entrance to each block which lies under the party wall, and the rhythm of the wide shop windows with their exposed steel lintels.

Opposite and to the south across carrer de Mallorca, the **passatge de Domingo** is a rare remaining cut through one of the *Eixample's* now built-up blocks.

88F Casa Pia Battló de Bach 1891–96

Gran Via de les Corts Catalanes/rambla de Catalunya

Josep Vilaseca i Casanovas

M Catalunya

On its prominent site facing the now impossibly traffic-choked Gran Via, and contemporary with Vilaseca's Casa Enric Battló i Battló **86**, this block of flats for another of the three brothers Battló was one of the first flagships of *Modernisme*. Vilaseca is now claimed as one of the founders of *Modernisme*, but his earlier domestic work never attains the full-bloodedness associated with that movement. He does manage to negotiate the corner via a pair of thin projecting towers surmounted by little lanterns, but the vertical composition is less assured than that of the Casa Enric Battló i Battló. The ceramic decoration is by Jaume Pujol i Bausis and the ironwork by Sancristòfol.

89| **Parc de Montjuïc** 1892–94, 1914, 1929, 1992

Josep Amargós i Samaranch, Puig i Cadafalch, Jean C.N. Forestier, Nicolau Rubió i Tudurí

M Espanya

The first castle **35** was built on Montjuïc at the end of the seventeenth century and its ramparts were extended in the eighteenth. The rest of the mountain remained as farmed private estates or as scrub. In the 1890s, Amargós, working for the association of the mountains' landowners, proposed the winding road which starts at the plaça Espanya and continues to the look-out at plaça Armada where the western terminus of the Transbordador is now located. It was intended to urbanise the area between this new road and the avinguda del Paral·lel below, but in 1908 the City bought one of the largest private estates and began to landscape it as the Parc Laribal. In 1914, the work on the Park was subsumed into that for **90F** the promotion of an International exhibition to be held in 1917 on the site. Puig i Cadafalch worked with Amargós on the layout for the Exhibition, and Puig re-ordered the plaça Espanya, and Amargós the avenue leading up the hill from it.

The Exhibition was postponed twice, but was eventually held in 1929. Meanwhile, Jean C.N. Forestier, the Parisian official gardener who had designed the Champ de Mars and restored parks at Seville between 1919 and 1922, was commissioned to lay out much of the slopes of the hill to the north of Amargós's road, and the Parc Laribal. Working with Nicolau Rubió i Tudurí, and using Mediterranean landscape and the Arabic gardens of Andalusia as examples, he consolidated the existing woodland and placed new features within it: monumental flights of steps, fountains and terraces all connected by winding paths. An old quarry was transformed into the Teatre Grec.

See also Plaça de Catalunya **144**, Poble Espanyol **145**, Palau Nacional **149**, and Font Màgica **148**.

Mercat de la Llibertat 1893

Plaça de la Llibertat, 186

Francesc Berenguer i Mestres

M Fontana

Gràcia was one of the settlements which through the building of the *Eixample* became connected to Barcelona proper. The market was built to serve the needs of what developed into a fashionable and expanding suburb where Berenguer, former pupil and collaborator of Gaudí, completed several buildings. The workmanlike iron structure of the roof shelters a main central hall flanked by aisles. The porch to the south, its gates, and the eaves brackets are decorated with art-nouveau flour-

ishes which, while correctly-swirling, are of a timidity suggesting that they might have been ordered from a catalogue.

Modernisme

91Jb Catalana de Gas i Electricitat 1895
Avinguda de Portal d'Angel, 20-22
Josep Domènech i Estapà

M Urquinaona

The architect of the contemporary Palau de Justícia **80** uses the same bombast in this monumental building to celebrate power of another kind. The language is Domènech i Estapà's own version of eclectic and slightly deranged Classicism, and his compositional principles are unclear, although the motif of the haunched segmental arch predominates in the façade.

92Jc Casa Martí *Els Quatre Gats* now Centre Cultural de la Caixa de Pensions 1895–96
Carrer de Montsió, 3 bis
Josep Puig i Cadafalch

M Catalunya

The earliest work by Puig i Cadafalch in Barcelona, started when he was only 28, has all the indications of his later mature style. A four-storey palace on a corner site, it is built of plain Roman brick. All the decoration is concentrated in the window surrounds with their eclectic variety of gothic elements culled from all over Europe and in the intense ironwork over the entrance. The continuous row of little arched windows on the top floor reoccurs throughout his later buildings.

At the beginning of the twentieth century, the *cerveseria* on the ground floor called *Els Quatre Gats* (Four Cats), now reopened as a restaurant, was at first a centre for cabaret and for Barcelona's *modernista* bohemian life, and later for the Christian Cercle Artístic de San Luc, whose members included Gaudí and the sculptor Llimona.

93F **Casa Thomas** 1895–98

Carrer de Mallorca, 291-293

Lluís Domènech i Montaner, Francesc Guàrdia i Vial

M Diagonal

Only the lower two storeys were designed by Domènech, originally for use as a small factory for the engraver Thomas. The ground floor workshop was lit by the very large arched window with its magnificent ironwork grille. In 1912 the building was turned into a standard *Eixample* block of flats when the three upper storeys were skilfully and seamlessly added by Guàrdia with Domènech's approval. The small, flanking rooftop towers, one Classical and the other Gothic, are paraphrases of those originally supplied lower down by Domènech.

94Ji **Duana nova (New Customs House)**
1895–1902

Passeig de Colom, 27/plaça del Portal de la Pau

Enric Sagnier i Villavecchia and Pere García Faria i Monteys

M Drassanes

By the end of the nineteenth century, the main focus of the activities of Barcelona's port had moved west from the plaça del Palau to the Portal de la Pau, leaving behind the old port offices and the previous Customs House, Duana vella **45**. This replacement is an office building in the form of an H-shaped palace and noteworthy for its roofline. The only excuses for the monstrously overscaled sculptures of winged sphinxes and the eagles on globes are either that *Modernisme* sanctioned excited rooflines, or that they might easily be seen from far out at sea.

Modernisme

95Jd **Hidroelèctrica de Catalunya** 1896–97

Avinguda de Vilanova, 12/carrer de Roger de Flor, 52

Pere Falqués i Urpi

M Arc de Triomf

Like Domènech i Estapà's Catalana de Gas i Electritat **91**, this building celebrates power, but separates the rhetorical gestures, confining them to the entrance to the offices on the corner, from the refreshingly tasteful machine hall to the east. The elevations of the hall are very carefully studied. The steel frame is exposed, supported on a stone base and filled with panels of orange brickwork which hold the arched windows, the whole capped by a Moorish battlemented top.

√ **96**F **Casa Amatller** now **Institut Amatller d'Art Hispànic** 1898–1900

Passeig de Gràcia, 41

Josep Puig i Cadafalch

M Passeig de Gràcia

Puig i Cadafalch's second work in Barcelona was a conversion for a chocolate manufacturer of an existing building, with the modifications being confined to the street side of the block. The massive façade of five bays is crowned by a large stepped gable decorated with tiles. Below this, and separated from it by Puig's characteristic strip of arched windows, the composition of five bays employs a pattern of intense patches of decoration round the doors and windows set against a ground of *esgrafiats* in ochre and white. The ironwork of the balconies and grilles is from the workshop of Pujol i Baucis. (Next door, to the north, is Gaudí's Casa Batlló **118**.)

97E **Plaça de Toros** *Les Arenes* 1899-1900

Plaça d'Espanya

August Font i Carreras

M Espanya

Of Barcelona's two remaining bullrings, this is the less architecturally distinguished (the other is the *Monumental* **129**). Its pretensions are limited to its moorish horseshoe arches and consistent detailing and are mocked by its present use as a car park and occasional venue for concerts.

98Jc **Casa Calvet** 1899–1900

Carrer de Casp, 48

Antoni Gaudí i Cornet

M Urquinaona

Of Gaudí's three buildings in the *Eixample*, this is the first (the others are the Casa Batlló **118** and the Casa Mila **119**). Built for the textile manufacturer Pedro Martin Calvet, it is conservative in both arrangement and style. At ground level there is a shop on either side of the entrance. Each of the four upper floors is planned round the central open stair and lift, and has two large flats which run through from front to back. There are four small light-wells which ventilate the rooms towards the middle of the plan. The regular flat but textured façade of five equally spaced bays is decorated with projecting balconies on bulbous brackets and is topped with two Dutch or baroque gables. The small-scale decoration is of naturalistic leaves, fruit and berries. On the ground floor not everything is so straightforward: the projecting 'columns' which separate the shops do not support anything, and the iron door-knocker to the front door has the Christian cross hammering an evil beetle. The shop to the right of the entrance should be noted for the extraordinary chasteness of its white brick walls and Catalan vaults of white tiles.

99A **Gate** 1900

Passeig de Manuel Girona, 57

Antoni Gaudí i Cornet

M Maria Cristina

Now restored, the arched and canopied gate set in a remnant of the boundary wall originally provided the entrance to the grounds of the Finca Mirralles, now occupied by Coderch's housing scheme 'Les Cotxeres de Sarrià', of 1973.

Modernisme

100B **Park Güell** 1900-14 (under restoration 1989–)
Carrer d'Olot

Antoni Gaudí i Cornet

Ⓜ Lesseps

The progressive industrialist Güell commissioned Gaudí to lay out a garden suburb. Both Güell's proposal and its spelling were possibly modelled on London's Bedford Park, started in 1875 and designed by Richard Norman Shaw and others.

What was built of Gaudí's layout surprisingly has little of the picturesque and artistic irregularity of that suburb and its arrangement is strikingly *beaux-arts*. The two bizarre and sumptuously-decorated entry lodges on carrer d'Olot, their elaborately profiled roofs clad in ceramics and designed to be seen from above, announce the beginning of an axis (the iron entry gates decorated with fan palms were originally installed at the Casa Vicens **68** and were removed here). This axis then rises up the hill via steps decorated with the famous and restored

ceramic dragon, and immediately provides the centre-line for the symmetrically arranged 'market hall', the park's largest building. The market has closely-spaced columns arranged on a square grid, each group of four supporting a small saucer dome faced with white broken ceramic. Gaudí uses an idiosyncratic version of the Doric order for the columns and their entablature, its traditional seriousness undermined by the columns' white 'leg-warmers', and by their inward inclination at the perimeter. The columns are hollow to allow rainwater from the terrace above to be drained into a reservoir behind the hall.

Above, the symmetrical terrace and roof of the market give fine views over eastern Barcelona, and its serpentine balustrade whose shape allows its patrons to face towards or away from each other is one of Gaudí 's most celebrated inventions. Prefabricated and installed in sections, it was decorated in brightly coloured broken ceramics by Gaudí's assistant and collaborator Josep María Jujol. Its final comfortable profile may have been determined by seating a naked workman in moist cement (architects now use handbooks of dimensions). Beyond the terrace, the axis fades away and on either side of it serpentine roads and paths give access to the more remote parts of the park. The paths are occasionally supported on or pass through arched and buttressed masonry retaining walls and viaducts in a variety of vegetable, mineral and and pseudo-structural forms to great picturesque effect. At the summit of the hill Gaudí had originally projected a chapel, but this was not built.

It was intended that the roads should provide access to sixty triangular plots for houses, but only two of these were built, including one by Francesc Berenguer i Mestres in 1904. This is reached from the straight promenade which extends to the east of the entrance lodges. Gaudí himself lived in this house from 1906 until his death in 1926, and it now houses a small museum. Güell died in 1918, and in 1922 the gardens passed to the city, since which time they have been a public park.

101B Casa Bellesguard 1900–02

Carrer Bellesguard, 16-20

Antoni Gaudí i Cornet

F Tibidabo

'Bellesguard' is the Catalan for 'Bellevue' and not the client's name: the house was commissioned by Dona Maria Sagués. The site was that of the ruins of a castle built in 1408 by the last king of Catalonia, Martí I. This seems to have influenced Gaudí's choice of forms, those of a compact battlemented castle from a fairy-tale, of a geometrical simplicity and of a restricted range of materials rare in his work. The walls and roof of the tall square house are entirely faced in rubble and dressed stone, the openings in which are extremely mannered versions of Catalan secular forms. The tripartite windows to the upper rooms are modelled on the Gothic, but the mullions are ridiculously elongated. The ceramic decoration on the wall in which the front door is placed are by Gaudí's assistant Sugrañes and were added after the house was finished. Supported by an elaborate, structurally daring and possibly improvised arrangement of brick piers, brick beams, tiled corbels and Catalan vaults, the roof is modelled to provide a promenade and look-out from behind the battlements. The house is private and rarely

accessible, but a glimpse may be had from the empty site to its south.

At carrer Bellesguard, 30 is the **Convent del Redemptor** of 1926 by Bernardi Martorell i Puig. Martorell's earlier convent, also nearby, is the Convent de Valldoncella **126** of 1910–19.

Modernisme

102E Casa Golferichs now Ajuntament de Barcelona Districte Eixample and Fundació Carles Pi i Sunyer 1900–01

Gran Via de les Corts Catalanes, 491/carrer de Viladomat

Joan Rubió i Bellver

M Urgell

Born in 1871, Bellver had been Gaudí's assistant between 1893 and 1905 when he worked on Sagrada Familia **76** and the Colònia Güell **XX**, but this was his first independent commission. The three-storey house for a single family occupies a corner site in the *Eixample*, built against its neighbours but with a small front yard approached through a roofed gate. It has carefully crafted rubble walls with crisp brick dressings to the Gothic windows, and the eaves and the gables facing the Gran Via are deeply overhung. See also Bellver's chapel of the Industrial University **62**, and the house *Frare Blanc* **111**.

103G Casa Macaya now Centre Cultural de la Caixa de Pensions 1901–02

Passeig de Sant Joan, 108

Josep Puig i Cadafalch

M Verdaguer

A near contemporary of Puig's Casa Amattler **96**, this grand house for a single family is arranged round a reinterpretation of the courtyard of a medieval merchant's house (see, e.g. carrer de Montcada **8**). From the courtyard, now protected by a modern roof, a covered stair lit by Moorish windows rises to the main rooms on the first floor. Of the original interior decoration, only that of the vestibule remains, decorated above the tiled base in yellow and white *esgrafiats* by Joan Paradís.

The organisation of the façade is nearly symmetrical: the two towers at the sides frame the composition. Against the expanse of white stucco there are exquisitely and intensely decorated stonework window surrounds. These are designed in varieties of late gothic and are placed in finely-judged asymmetry topped by Puig's characteristic arcade of banded windows. The subjects of the sculptured decoration by Eusebi Arnau are not limited to the medieval, for they include a portrayal of the bicycle which conveyed Puig to site visits.

Both this house and much of Puig's later work transcend the narrower concerns of *Modernisme*, and hint at the timeless 'Mediterraneanism' which has had such an international appeal. He lived until 1957, and it is surprising that he was never tempted to Hollywood.

104F **Casa Jeroni F. Granell** 1901–03
Passeig de Girona, 122
Jeroni Ferran Granell i Manresa

M Verdaguer

The architect himself acted as promoter and client for these flats which became one of the many textbook developments in the *Eixample*. Above the stone-faced semi-basement and ground floor each of the five storeys is of equal height: there is no *piano nobile*. There are two flats per floor which run from front to back, ventilated by light wells placed against the party walls. Set against the façade, decorated in delicate *esgrafiats* of green ivy against a lilac ground, the windows are topped with stylised pine-cones, and have Granell's characteristic softly moulded, curved surrounds. These are echoed in the waves of the sinusoidal cornice.

105 Jc **Cases Joaquim Cabot** 1901–04
Carrer Roger de Llúria, 8-10, 12-14
Josep Vilaseca i Casanovas

M Urquinaona

The development of these two sites by same client at the same time gave Vilaseca the opportunity for his first essay in thoroughgoing *Modernisme*. Numbers 8-10, of six bays, are the more conventional. The windows are grouped vertically and topped by a cheerful curly medieval feature. The surround to the front door is successfully eclectic, and the decorations of the entrance hall are intact. To the north, numbers 12–14, of four bays, are faced in salmon and pale green *esgrafiats* and have very prominent glazed balconies which, while augmenting the built space, are more usually found at the back on the inside of the block.

Modernisme

106G **Hospital de Sant Pau** 1901–10, 1930
Carrer de Sant Antoni Maria Claret, 167-171/
carrer de Cartagena
Lluís Domènech i Montaner

M Hospital de Sant Pau

This hospital was built by the bequest of the banker
Pau Gil to replace the old hospital of Santa Creu **19**
which until then had been the only one serving
Barcelona. It gave Domènech his greatest opportunity to put into practice the *modernista* programme, and this building, together with his Palau
de la Música Catalana **117**, are the most important
monuments of that movement. In 1912, Domènech
retired from work on the hospital, and after his
death in 1923, his son Pere continued to complete
the work. All the wards were finally transferred
from Santa Creu by 1930.

The hospital is laid out on a sloping site of nine
blocks, the buildings arranged around its diagonal
axis so that they mostly face south. The difficulty
with this arrangement is that it is more appropriate
to a suburban rather than an urban site, and the
buildings nearer the edges present their corners
either to each other or to the surrounding streets.
The administration building at the lowest, southern, corner, its wings or arms outstretched, provides the main and symbolic entrance.

This is the most complete example of Domènech's
attempt to harness all the arts and crafts to make
a complete art-work, to make architecture 'speak',
and all the prominent artists, sculptors, mosaicists,
and metalworkers were employed to decorate the
finely crafted brick buildings. Beyond entrance and
half-way up the slope and at the top are the central
buildings housing the operating theatres, laborato-
ries and kitchen. Regularly and symmetrically arranged on either side of the axis, the long ward
blocks present their pavilioned ends to the central
open space. These are complete buildings in
themselves. The domed and elaborately decorated circular pavilions contain a day room and
mark the entrance. Beyond the domes are the
open wards, and at the end of each block is a group
of private rooms. The whole complex is served by
a complete system of underground corridors which
connects all the buildings together.

The street which cuts diagonally across the grid
connecting the hospital to the site of the Sagrada
Família, now the **Avinguda de Gaudí**, was re-
ordered in 1988 (Màrius Quintana, architect,
Ajuntament de Barcelona), with re-cast lamp
standards by Pere Falqués and sculptures by
Apel·les Fenosa.

107F Casa Lamadrid

Carrer Girona, 113

Lluís Domènech i Montaner

M Verdaguer

This is Domènech's only essay in a standard development in the *Eixample* (the other two, the palau Ramon de Montaner **79** and casa Thomas **93**, were exceptional), and its form is largely determined by municipal by-laws. The narrow plot has commerce on the ground floor and five floors of flats above. The two through flats on each floor are planned around two central light wells, one of which lights and ventilates the stairs. The façade is composed of a regularly repeated single window, each framed withthin columns which support the balcony above. These project from the almost flat surface of the monochrome stone façade which is relieved by a pattern of very delicately carved horizontal bands and raised medallions. The whole is topped by a fretted cornice with a single battlement in the centre. At the ground floor the architecture is more robust and the shops are separated from the entrance by beefy columns with cabbage rose capitals. The entrance hall and stairs retain their original decoration.

108F Casa Llopis Bofill 1902–03

Carrer de València, 339/carrer de Bailén, 113

Antoni Gallissà i Soqué

M Verdaguer

Gallissà collaborated with Domènech i Montaner on the Café-Restaurant **81** for the 1888 exhibition and in the craft workshop established there after the exhibition closed. But in this, his most important work, completed in the year of his death in 1903, he shed the medievalism of the previous decade. The near-triangular site is on a corner of an *Eixample* block and has very short returns to the streets on either side. Planned around a central stair there are two flats on each floor, each with its own light well against the party wall. The elevations are notable for the cantilevered and stacked glazed balconies which replace those normally found at the back of the building, but which are not possible here because there is very little 'back' in the internal corner of the block. Between the rectangular balconies, the walls are flat expanses of cream stucco decorated with floral and geometrical *esgrafiats*. The façades are supported on brick arches whose stone columns divide the commercial accommodation on the ground floor. The top of the building has been slightly altered: what was originally a horizontal storey of banded brick has since been stuccoed, giving a more vertical emphasis to the composition.

Modernisme

109F **Casa Terrades, 'Casa de les Punxes'**
1903–05
Avinguda Diagonal, 416-420/carrer del Rosselló
260-262
Josep Puig i Cadafalch
M Verdaguer

This is one of Barcelona's most popular and well-known buildings and *Casa de les Punxes* is its affectionate nickname. On an irregular pentagonal island, the result of slicing the avinguda Diagonal through Cerdà's regular square grid, the development was commissioned by three sisters of the Terrades family. The building is divided into three blocks of flats, but the planning of each floor is extremely complex: the most ordered section is towards carrer del Rosselló, but the rest succumbs to angled disorder.

Round towers negotiate the corners of the site, each crowned with a spire. The tower on the sharp corner to avinguda Diagonal is a storey higher than the rest and given more elaborate decoration, including corbelled eaves. Between the military towers are flat gabled façades modelled on central European medieval domestic architecture. Each is composed as a single house with a stone arcade below, brick above, and all the applied elements have a diminutive scale. The façade to carrer del Rosselló is the most coherent composition, its central gable decorated with a mosaic panel showing St George, patron saint of Catalonia. The building's stone carving and sculpture are by Alfons Juyol and the ironsmith was Manuel Ballerín.

110F **Casa Serra** 1903–08
Rambla de Catalunya, 126/avinguda Diagonal
Josep Puig i Cadafalch
M Diagonal

Of Puig's work, only the façades and the entrance hall remain. The house was never lived in by its client and shortly after completion it was converted for use as a convent. Redevelopment was threatened in the 1960s, but total demolition was prevented by a popular campaign. Left to admire are the two beautifully restored suave façades hinged on the projecting tower, their surfaces adorned with carefully placed windows and the superb carving to the front door, all decorated with finely-carved Renaissance profiles. The tower and the roof with its restored polychrome tilework are reminders of Puig's medievalism.

The newer grey offices which have been built behind the house, their shape and round corner towers perhaps echoing those of Puig, were completed in 1987 (architects Frederic Correa i Riuz, X. Garido i Langunilla, A. Mila i Sagnier and F. Ribas i Barrangé). They are now occupied by the Disputació de Barcelona.

111B **Restaurant *Asador de Aranda* formerly Casa Roviralta *(Frare Blanc)*** 1903–13

Avinguda de Tibidabo, 31

Joan Rubió i Bellver

F Tibidabo

The house was built on a site promoted by the Societat Anónima del Tibidabo, at the turn of the century developers of the land on either side of the avinguda del Tibidabo which runs north from the end of the carrer de Balmes to the funicular station at the foot of the mountain. The route was popularised by the *tramvia blau* ('blue tram', but at present a blue bus) whose lines ran along it. The company wished to develop a garden city of individual houses on large plots, and the casa Roviralta was built on part of the site of a former convent of the Dominicans, the Frare Blanc (white friars).

The plan is free and generous, presenting to the street a gabled wing to the right of which the entrance is placed. Beyond this is another long wing whose whole top storey is an open loggia, its

gable facing towards the avinguda de Tibidabo. The exterior displays Bellver's most intense involvement with *Modernisme*, with its combination of Catalan and Moorish features in brick placed against a flat white ground. The skill of the bricklayers is remarkable: note particularly the cantilevered thin courses of tile which protect the eaves, and the decorated balustrades and window heads. The restaurant specialises in grilled meat and its sumptuously decorated dining rooms can be visited.

112F **Casa Quadras, now Museu de la Música** 1904–06

Avinguda Diagonal, 373/carrer del Rosselló, 279

Josep Puig i Cadafalch

M Diagonal

On a trapezoidal site between avinguda Diagonal and carrer del Rosselló, this was a substantial conversion for the baron de Quadras of an earlier house. The reorganised accommodation was placed to the north, arranged round a central patio and with its new entrance from avinguda Diagonal. Designed to suggest a single house, this façade has the more elaborate and medievalising architecture. Its most conspicuous feature is the intensively decorated gallery which, supported on brackets, extends for the full width, as does the row of flat-arched windows under the eaves. The superb stone carving is by Eusebi Arnau and the ironwork by Manuel Ballerín. The interiors are disappointing and their decoration shows little of the subtlety of the exterior.

The elevation to carrer del Rosselló presents an amalgam of the front and back of a block of flats. The ground floor suggests and contains an entrance, while the plain glazed balconies above are more usually found on the inside of the block.

Modernisme

113F **Hospital Clínic** 1904
Carrer Casanova, 143
Josep Domènech i Estapà
M Hospital Clínic

On a special site of two standard *Eixample* blocks interrupting carrer del Rosselló, the ward buildings run north and south from the central and axial block. This latter has a portico surmounted by a lumpy broken pediment containing sculpture. If the Hospital de Sant Pau **106** represents a radically nationalistic and, in the articulation of its parts, a rational and humanistic tradition, the Hospital Clínic represents the opposites. It is monolithic, built of 'official' stone, uses a stripped down and distorted classical language to impress or intimidate. Even its orthogonal axis compared with the forty-five degrees of Sant Pau's can be read as oppressive. Domènech i Estapà's buildings are presently disused, but the work of the modern hospital continues, its entrance in carrer de Villarroel.

114B **Fabra Observatory** 1904
Tibidabo
Josep Domènech i Estapà
F Tibidabo

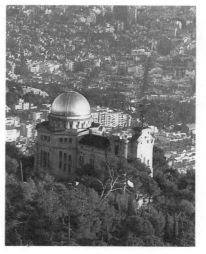

One of the institutions which include Sagnier's Science Museum **202** built in conjunction with the development of the avinguda del Tibidabo and the funicular, the observatory was the gift to the city of the marquès d'Alella.

115F Cases Castillo Villanueva 1904–09

Carrer Roger de Lluria, 80/carrer de Valencia, 312

Juli Fossas i Martínez

Ⓜ Passeig de Gràcia

These two blocks were built at the same time and originally formed a symmetrical composition on the diagonal corner. The northerly block has been altered and its elaborate balconies and rococo tower removed. The southerly oblique corner remains, however, and the droopy, bony structure of the balconies is a reminder that the bones of Gaudí's contemporary Casa Batlló **118** were not unique. The distinctly *moderniste* balconies are set against the severe façades, the whole composition suggesting a tension between *Modernisme* and the emerging *Noucentisme*.

116F Casa Lleó Morera 1905

Passeig de Gràcia, 35

Lluís Domènech i Montaner

Ⓜ Diagonal

This house afforded Domènech the opportunity to carry out one of his most ambitious essays in harnessing all the arts and crafts to a domestic architectural programme. All the famous and fashionable artist-artisans of the day were employed, including the stone-carver Eusebi Arnau, the sculptor Alfons, ceramicist Antoni Serra i Fiter and mosaicist Lluís Bru (Arnau, who infiltrated Puig's bicycle to the 'medieval' carving of the Casa Macaya **104**, here introduces a gramophone, a telephone and a camera).

The legibility of the façades was destroyed when the building was cruelly altered in 1943 by introducing the present continuous shopfront. This removed what photographs show to have been the building's springy and elegant connection with the ground, and some of Arnau's best carving. Much of the interior's original furniture has been preserved and is now housed in museums, but many of the interiors are intact, including the vestibule with mosaics by Lluís Bru who also decorated the exterior cupola with its green, yellow, pink and white tilework.

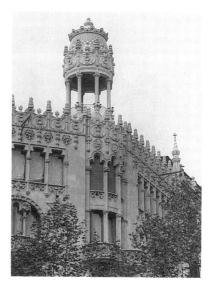

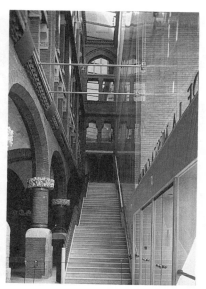

117 Jc **Palau de la Música Catalana** 1905–08

Plaça d'Amadeu Vives, 1/carrer de Sant Pere
més alt, 11

*Lluís Domènech i Montaner; extensions 1982-
90, Oscar Tusquets, Studio Per*

M Urquinaona

The Orfeó Català, a private choral society, was
founded by Lluís Millet in 1891, and the Palau was
built as its permanent home for its performances
of popular Catalan music and works from the
standard orchestral repertoire. Surprisingly, it was
not located in the *Eixample*, but on an irregular and
cramped site near the newly opened via Laietana.
The building consists of a masonry outer wall
inside which is a steel frame which supports the
stalls and the cantilevered balconies of a standard
U-shaped auditorium. The floor of the auditorium is
at first floor level supported by a regular grid of
columns and vaults. Below it, and entered directly
off the street (and originally only from the north-
east corner), is the vestibule with its monumental
double stair, and beyond this a bar and promenade. All the main internal partitions, including the
screens which separate the auditorium from its
surrounding circulation areas, are of glass. Even
the uprights of all the balustrades in the building
are of yellow glass cylinders.

The building is both the consummation of the entire
modernista programme and the triumph of
Domènech's career. In his mid-fifties, he was able
to use the experience of thirty years finally to
produce a total art work devoted to the nationalistic cause. Those who feel uneasy with a hospital's
being used as a vehicle for artistic ideology
(Domènech's Hospital de Sant Pau **106**) may be
persuaded by the dedication of all the plastic arts
to the celebration of music. The musical connection is direct: Wagner was one of the ideologues
admired by the proponents of *Modernisme*, and his
concept of the total art work (the *gesamtkunstwerk*)
was central to their programme. Wagner is celebrated in one of the two allegorical sculptures by
Pau Gargallo which mark the division between
audience and stage and seep across the ceiling to
form an approximation to a proscenium. That on
the left shows the *Ride of the Valkyrie*, who erupt
from the top of a Roman Doric order which frames
a bust of Beethoven, while on the right is the
thrusting tree of Catalan national identity among
whose branches is found a bust of Anselm Clavé,
reviver and promoter of Catalan popular music.

The bones of Domènech's architecture are the
tough masonry and steel construction, brick piers
with capitals of ceramic cabbage roses, brick
arches, and both Catalan and groined vaults.
Among the artists harnessed to the decorative
scheme were the sculptors Miquel Blay who made
the sculpture on the exterior corner which is dedicated to popular song and Francisco Modolell. Eusebio
Arnau who carved the upper parts of the Muses who
emerge from their painted lower halves to decorate
the walls of the back of the stage. The sumptuous
mosaic decoration inside and out is by Lluís Bru, and
the glass is by the Rigalt Granell Company.

The spirited extensions of the 1980s slightly enlarged the seating capacity of the hall, and opened up the site to the north-west by demolishing part of the church next door. A new entrance lobby was provided from which a new stair rises outside the original perimeter of the building to augment the original stair at the front. The bar was spruced up and given beautiful new minimalist lighting. On the northern side of the new entrance yard is a wing of accommodation for the Orfeó's administration, and this is marked by the circular turret which now signals the building to via Laietana.

The Palau and the Liceu **54** are Barcelona's only venues for performances of large-scale classical music and will remain so until the projected National Auditorium **222** by Rafael Moneo is built. To visit the interior of the Palau, brave the near-impenetrable booking arrangements and the paranoid management and go to a performance.

118F Casa Batlló 1905–07

Passeig de Gràcia, 43

Antoni Gaudí i Cornet

M Diagonal

The textile manufacturer José Batlló i Casanovas commissioned this reconstruction of an earlier building of 1875. Gaudí added the top floor and completely remodelled the first floor and the access to it. He added a new façade to match the height and grandeur of Puig i Cadafalch's Casa Amatller **96** to the south. The visible internal work includes the lift and stair well, whose width and blueness of its tiled decoration both increase as it progresses up the building. The well is covered with a rooflight supported on parabolic I-beams. The main suite of rooms on the first floor was planned so far as the constraint of the parallel crosswalls would allow in Gaudí's 'cellular' style. The shape of each room seems to have been determined by a process in which each space was treated like a soap bubble whose final form only emerged as the result of 'pressure' from its neighbours. This planning technique reached its apotheosis in the much larger scale of Casa Milà **119**. The rooms were extensively decorated with plasterwork by Josep Maria Jujol i Gilbert, and with the panelling, and fixed and movable furniture designed by Gaudí and others, much of it now in museums (some in the museum at Park Güell **100**), and all showing the same viscous tendencies.

The exterior presents the ceramic-faced symbols of St George and the dragon. On no other building has such a palette been used: deep blue, purple, green, ochre and brown tiles cover all the floors above the first, and then extend over the roof whose humped ridge is that of the dragon's back. The decorative scheme is Jujol's. To Salvador Dalí the façade suggested the shining iridescence of the 'tranquil waters of a lake'. The building faces north-east, and its reflectivity celebrates the morning sun. The larger windows are towards the base of the building, and those on the upper storeys have individual iron balconies shaped ominously in

the form of skulls. The first floor bay window whose glass is decorated with coloured panels and roundels is carried out in the cellular pattern. Stone dribbles from its sill like frozen saliva to form the bony frame to the ground floor which supports the building and surrounds the shopfitting.

119F Casa Milà ('La Pedrera') 1905–11
Passeig de Gràcia, 92/carrer de Provença
Antoni Gaudí i Cornet and Enric Sagnier

Ⓜ Diagonal

Gaudí's last building before he retired to devote the rest of his life to the Temple de la Sagrada Família was this speculative block of flats for Batlló's partner Don Pedro Milá. It is a large building on an ample prominent site on the corner of a typical *Eixample* block. The plot is not symmetrical, and its longer arm extends along carrer de Provença, giving some frontage to the light and air available on the inside of the block. The floors are planned around two polygonal light wells which light the kitchens and corridors, and each flat is a complete essay in the 'bubble' or 'cellular' planning of rooms which Gaudí first developed in the Casa Batlló. This is made possible by the building's heterogeneous structure, a mixture of loadbearing masonry and a steel frame.

The first scheme had a single light well with a continuous ramp for vehicles which would have been able to reach the front door of each flat. This arrangement was abandoned, and now there is only a ramp down to the basement (like that of the Palau Güell **78**). A further organisational innovation was, however, retained. The lifts and stairs are not clumped together but separated to serve different ends of each flat, the lift arriving at the front door and the stair at the 'back' for the servants.

The marine metaphor for the exterior of the building bears no relation to its nickname 'La Pedrera' ('The Quarry'). The undulating white masonry which covers the highly irregular steel frame may be a cliff or a frozen wave. Its continuous lines are horizontal, each floor level being marked by a projecting sharp edge. The modelling of the surfaces in between is smooth and the openings in it irregular (window openings frequently do not coincide vertically), so that the emphasis is finally horizontal. The iron seaweed, designed by Jujol, which has caught against the balustrades of the balconies is certainly literally modelled, and the turquoise hexagonal tiles which Gaudí designed to decorate the pavements surrounding the building have an explicit nautical theme with their starfish and octopuses. (These tiles are still being made and their use extended to all the pavements of the Passeig de Gràcia.)

The building Gaudí designed was higher than the bylaws allowed, and the large top floor which he intended to cover with polychrome decoration with a religious theme was eventually cased in unremarkable diagonally laid white tiles. This attic has a special structure of thin diaphragm walls pierced by parabolic arches. Above its undulating eaves are the sculpted finials of chimneys and ventilation stacks which are decorated with violently coloured glass, ceramics and mosaics, part of the extraordinary landscape of the roof, from which the view to the north-east includes the spires of the Temple of the Sagrada Família.

120A **Casa Sastre Marqués** 1905
Carrer d'Eduard Conde, 44
Josep Puig i Cadafalch

F Reina Elisenda

Puig designed both pharmacist Sastre's shop at carrer del Hospital, 109, and this, his home. The shop is decayed, but the house was saved from demolition in 1973. It is announced from the corner of its site by the gazebo with its turreted and tiled witch's-hat roof. Its garden façade of three storeys is now almost hidden by dense foliage, and is gabled like a chalet, but the architecture of the return to carrer Cardenal Vives Tutó is more mixed. Here the ground floor is faced with turquoise and white tiles whose windows have fine ironwork grilles, while the white stucco above is capped with Moorish brick battlements, and Puig's trademark, the clerestory under the eaves, reappears.

121F **Casa Heribert Pons** now **Generalitat de Catalunya Department d'Economia i Finances** 1907–09
Rambla de Catalunya, 19-21
Alexander Soler i March

M Catalunya

This is an early work of Soler, and one of the few in Barcelona: his later work is mostly elsewhere. He was a pupil of Domènech i Montaner but here ventured well beyond his master's nationalistic eclecticism. His sources for this large block of flats are Viennese, particularly Otto Wagner's Anker Insurance building of 1893–95. While both the interior and outside of the block have frequently been altered, the façade and vestibule were last restored in 1978 to repair bomb damage of 1938. The façade employs a Wagnerian tall central feature flanked by flat piers (which have lost their finials), while further piers mark the party walls. The lumpy details are relieved by the sculptures of Eusebio Arnau who also made the statue of Diana in the vestibule.

The Rambla de Catalunya is rich in architecture. To the north of this house at number 23 is the **Casa Jaume Moysi** of 1895 by Manuel Comas i Thois, and further north again number 27, the **Casa Climent Arola** finished in 1902 by Francesc de Pau del Villar i Carmona.

Modernisme

122F Casa Fuster 1908–10
Passeig de Gràcia, 132
Lluís Domènech i Montaner

M Passeig de Gràcia

This is the latest work by Domènech to be included in this book: there is little subsequent important work up to his death in 1923. The prominent and irregular site is at the northmost extent of the *Eixample,* where the wide passeig de Gràcia finishes and joins the older narrower road, the Gran via de Gràcia. The composition is similar to that of Domènech's Casa Lleó Morera **116**, with a round tower used at the corner, here clad in bands of pink and white marble. The decorative motifs of the façades make an uneasy compendium of Domènech's usages of a lifetime, with the Classical predominating below and including the projecting screen at first-floor level, while towards the top small, possibly Venetian Gothic forms emerge to break the skyline. The return face away from the passeig de Gràcia is much plainer.

123F Casa Rubinat 1909
Carrer Or, 44
Francesc Berenguer i Mestres

M Fontana

A pupil of Gaudí, Berenguer died, prematurely, in 1914, before his master. This block of flats is his last major work. The façade of four bays is completely regular, each separate window having its own fine wrought-iron balcony. The only departures are on the commercial ground floor where four arches with triangular heads carry the masonry above, and at the skyline where the windows on the top floor are capped by triangular hoods with spires both in brick. The stucco between the windows has fine *esgrafiat* decoration.

The block faces the **parc de la Virreina** to the north. This was designed by Jaume Bach and Gabriel Mora, and was an early scheme of the city's parks programme of the 1980s.

124F Casa Comalat 1909–11
Avinguda Diagonal, 442/carrer de Còrsega, 316
Salvador Valeri i Pupurull
M Diagonal

The site extends north from avinguda Diagonal to emerge on the corner of carrer de Còrsega and carrer Roger de Llúria, giving the block two façades. The more formal front, in cheerful fruity Baroque, faces avinguda Diagonal. But at the back and usually hidden from view are the continuous glazed balconies with pretty tiled spandrels, the whole treated with the faceted abandon necessary to get the ensemble round the obliquely-angled corner. It is supported on a bony masonry frame and topped with a bulging and thickly scrolled cornice which curves in all three dimensions.

125F Monument to Doctor Robert 1910
Plaça de Tetuan
Josep Limona, sculptor
M Girona

Doctor Bartomeu Robert was a popular mayor of Barcelona, and this is his civic monument raised by public subscription. Above a basin and supported on four stumpy columns is a dome or small mountain, or a mushroom head, from the top of which emerges a conventional bust of Dr Robert. Clambering up the sloping sides are allegorical groups of figures in bronze. Domènech i Montaner was originally associated with the project, but never produced a design. The forms and the white stone are so similar to those of the contemporary Casa Milà **119** that an attribution to Gaudí is irresistible, and while the sculptor Limona was a friend and one of his close collaborators, but there is no documentary evidence of Gaudí's involvement. The monument originally stood in the plaça Universitat, but was dismantled during the Civil War. It was re-erected on the present site in 1985, in its new landscaped setting designed by A. Arriola of the Ajuntament de Barcelona.

Modernisme

126B Convent de Valldoncella 1910–19

Carrer Cister, 41

Bernardi Martorell i Puig

F Tibidabo

One of the two convents by Martorell in the neighbourhood, this was built for a Cistercian order on a suburban site after the destruction in 1909 of an earlier home in central Barcelona. The church of the new convent was finally consecrated in 1923, but during the Civil War the whole building was converted and used as anti-tuberculosis sanitorium. The church has a plan in the form of a Latin cross and is entered through a parabolic arch in the base of the square tower set in the crook of the cross. Beyond the church and to the south-west is a large cloister of three storeys, the top one of which provides the convent's main and private circulation. The construction shows the influence of both Domènech i Montaner in its tough red brickwork and the brutal gables which break the roof line, and of Gaudí in the parabolic arches of the windows and nave of the tall church.

127Je Església del Carme and **Escuela Parroquial** 1910–14, 1930–49

Carrer del Bisbe Laguarda/carrer Sant Antoni Abat

Josep M. Pericas i Morros

M Sant Antoni

The earlier church on the site was destroyed in Semana Trágica in 1909, and while its replacement was started in 1913, it was not finished until 1930. The campanile was added in 1949. The brick church presents four bays of the flank of its tall nave to the street, each bay indicated by a gable, and its windows grouped and set in battered frames. Below are the gables of the side chapels. The curiously unplaced style owes little to *Modernisme*, but more perhaps to contemporary developments in Amsterdam. The highly decorated interior is designed to a scheme by Darius Vilàs. The parish school is fitted on to the rest of the site and continues the composition round the corner to carrer Sant Antoni Abat. (Most of Pericas's work is outside Barcelona, but he also designed the Monument to Jacint Verdaguer **130**.)

128I Fàbrica Cassaramona (yarn factory) now
Police Barracks 1910–11

Carrer de Mèxic, 36-44

Josep Puig i Cadafalch

Ⓜ Espanya

Much of the wealth of nineteenth-century Barcelona was made from the textile trade, but apart from this factory few architecturally significant industrial monuments were built or have been preserved. This factory remains, and is one of Puig's few non-domestic buildings in Barcelona, and his last to show any remaining allegiance to *Modernisme*. (By the 1920s he had rediscovered the baroque and his subsequent work is Classical, for example the palaus de Alfonso XIII i de Victoria Eugenia of 1923-28 at Montjuïc **143**.)

Three parallel ranges of buildings occupy a whole *Eixample* block. One of the two outer ranges was for spinning yarn, the other for weaving it. They are marked at the corners with an extra storey. The various buildings in the central range were for offices and services, their axis marked at either end by a water tower. The towers are used for advertisement and are of complex form decorated with pinnacles clad in ceramics. The ensemble has a diminutive scale, and this and the decorative cornice of *mudéjar* battlements give the factory the air of a child's toy fort. The construction is, however, strictly utilitarian: the loadbearing exterior masonry encloses manufacturing halls whose roofs are supported by a grid of steel columns. The building was taken over by the national guard in 1936 and has been occupied by the police ever since. Puig's 'fort' found appropriate occupants.

Ceramic pavement tiles in passeig de Gràcia, to a design by Antoni Gaudí i Cornet

Moderne to modern 1911–39

129G **Plaça de Toros *Monumental*** 1913–16

Gran Via de les Corts Catalanes, 749

Ignasi Mas i Morell (Joaquim Raspall i Mayol)

M Glòries

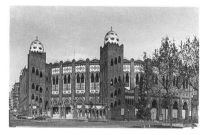

Of Barcelona's two remaining bull rings, this is the larger and the more architecturally assured. The other is the *Las Arenas* **97**. The building we now see is actually an extension and refacing of a ring finished only a few years earlier, and it now occupies a single *Eixample* block, its main entrance angled towards the south-west corner. Its eight stair towers are fitted neatly into the spaces left over between the circle of the arena and the square of the block, and their plans are twisted to align with the surrounding streets rather than following the geometry of the arena. The exterior is very spirited, with finely modelled brickwork and startlingly bright blue and white ceramic cladding, the whole an apparently effortless synthesis of Gothic and *mudéjar* elements. The garishly decorated and fanciful egg-shaped domes which terminate the stair towers are particularly remarkable and probably unprecedented.

130F **Monument to Jacinto Verdaguer** 1913–24

Passeig de Sant Joan/avinguda Diagonal

Josep M. Pericas i Morros

M Verdaguer

One of the two works in Barcelona by the prolific Pericas, the monument in cream stone is a stumpy and unclassical column surmounted by a statue of the nineteenth-century poet who, with Maragall, helped develop a modern literature in Catalan. It is surrounded by a stone stockade with sculpture by the brothers Oslé, and the stylistic models are exclusively Viennese. (See also Pericas's Església del Carme **127**)

Moderne to modern

131F Casa Ferrer-Vidal 1914–16
Passeig de Gràcia, 114
Eduard Ferrés i Puig

M Diagonal

The building has been altered and its original
terminal dome removed. Like that of the Casa
Heribert Pons **121**, the classical composition of the
façade, the 1:3:1 rhythm of its bays, is clearly
influenced by the Viennese work of Otto Wagner.
There are three floors for commercial uses, the top
one marked by the huge segmental arch which
bulges forward across the three central bays, its
shape repeated in the residential balcony on the
seventh floor.

132Jk Edificio Correros/Palau Comunicacions
1914–27
Via Laietana, 1/plaça d'Antonio López, 1
Josep Goday i Casals and Jaume Torres i Grau

M Barceloneta

This building, one of a contemporary series of post
offices erected in all Spain's important cities, also
celebrated the completion of the via Laietana, the
broad street cut through medieval Barcelona to
link the *Eixample* with the port. Its monumentality
is that of the state rather than the city, and it owes
nothing to *Modernisme*. It is rather one of the
earlier and larger examples of *Noucentisme*, the
classicising tendency and reaction to what were
caricatured as the parochial excesses of
Modernisme. Artists of the tendency were employed to decorate the huge entrance hall and
included Canyellas, Obiols and Galí i Labarta.
Goday was later employed on Barcelona's extensive school building programme.

133F Conservatorio Superior Municipal de Mùsica (Conservatory of Music) 1916–28

Carrer Valencia, 330/carrer Bruc, 104-112

Antoni de Falguera Sivilla

M Girona

A late *modernista* work, the building relies heavily on Puig i Cadafalch's techniques for the architecture of the corner and uses the same lower flat façades hinged round the taller and turreted towers (see for example Puig's Casa Terrades **109**). The association between the two architects is not surprising: Falguera was, with Goday and Puig, one of the co-editors of the history *L'arquitectura romànica a Catalunya* published between 1909 and 1918. Falguera lacked Puig's exquisite decorative taste, however, and while in the central bay he uses Puig's continuous arcade under the roof, the remaining openings are treated perfunctorily and the results are cheerless. The exception is Eusebi Arnau's decorative panel over the front door. The interior is notable for its tall central space which can be used for performances.

34Jc Teatro Tívoli 1917–19

Carrer de Casp, 6

Miquel Madorell i Ruis

M Urquinaona

Barcelona's only purpose-built theatre, started in 1905 by architect Madorell i Ruis, continued by others, and finally finished by Madorell. It opened in 1919 just in time for the arrival of the cinema. Occupying much of the north side of the block, the bland four-storey façade with large regular windows suggests that it could be an office building. Although the outside has been much altered we can still admire the delicacy of the glass canopy and of the ground floor's Ionic columns. The internal spaces for circulation are as grandly planned as those of an opera house and for a social ritual now largely abandoned. In 1990 the building was acquired by a new owner who plans to turn it into a multiplex cinema. See also the Cine Coliseo **142** of 1923.

Moderne to modern

135 Jc **Caixa de Pensions buildings** 1917–19
Via Laietana, 56–58 and carrer Jonqueres, 2
Eric Sagnier i Villavecchia

M Urquinaona

The construction of the via Laietana at the beginning of the twentieth century made available for modern enterprises large sites which were still surrounded by the medieval city. The *Eixample* was originally, as it remains today, mainly residential. The Post Office building **132** and the Baixeras school **136** marked the southern end of the street, and the two headquarters buildings for the bank were the most substantial at the northern. All of them were affected by *Noucentisme*, the reaction to *Modernisme*. While this reaction usually took the form of a *rappel à l'ordre*, a return to a Mediterranean or an international Classicism, Sagnier has here continued the medievalising thread of *Modernisme*, but using Nordic rather than local sources. The huge, artfully asymmetrical gothic frontispiece with its fine, complex corner tower and huge three-storey high pointed window dominates the via Laietana. The sculpture on the much more conventional return to the north is by Manuel

Fuxà. The office building to the east on the corner of carrer Jonqueres is much less showy, and its rational form and repetitive narrow bays suggest that Sagnier was familiar with the modern office planning of contemporary North America, of Chicago or New York. Decoration is restricted almost entirely to the roofline, although the sculpture over the door is attributed to the ubiquitous Eusebi Arnau, whose reputation survived the demise of *Modernisme*.

136 Jg **Col·legi Públic *Baixeras* (school)** 1918–22
Via Laietana, 11
Josep Goday i Casals

M Barceloneta

The particular contribution of Goday to Barcelona's ambitious and progressive school building programme in the first quarter of the twentieth century is described in the Introduction. This example is shoehorned on to the tight irregular site produced by the collision of the line of the via Laietana with the medieval street pattern to the west. The planning is extremely economical. A single large stair at the southern corner provides access to the five floors of stacked classrooms which are arranged around a central social space and accessible without the need for corridors. The block is punctured by two small light wells. Goday's brand of etiolated Mediterraneanism seems to have been no help in proportioning storey-heights, and in this the Baixeras school is no more successful than his others. It is stuccoed, and 'beautified' by *esgrafiat* panels of disagreeable sentimentality, with illustrations of prancing little girls on the lower floors and inconsequential vases of flowers above. Only the correct Tuscan main door preserves architectural propriety. See also the contemporary schools *Milà i Fontanals* **137**, *Ramon Llull* **139** and *Pere Vila* **140**, and the later **158** *Collasso i Gil* of 1932.

137 Je **Col·legi Públic *Milà i Fontanals* ex *Vicens Vives* (school)** 1919–21

Carrer del Carme, 80/carrer dels Angels

Josep Goday i Casals

M Liceu

A single block set back from the street decorated in very plain rococo stucco on a stone base. Only the large windows and high ceilings identify it as as school. See also Goday's contemporary schools *Baixeras* **136**, *Ramon Llull* **139**, and Pere Vila **140**, and the later *Collasso i Gil* **158** of 1932.

138A **Palau de Pedralbes** now **Museu de les Arts Decoratives** 1919–29

Avinguda Diagonal, 686

Eusebi Bona i Puig and Frances de Pau Nebot i Torrens; garden by Nicolau Maria Rubió i Tudurí 1925

M Palau Reial

Work began in 1919 to convert an existing building in what had been part of Eusebio Güell's estate into a palace for the Royal Family, but it was not finished when Alfonso XIII stayed there in 1926. By 1929, however, and in time for the International Exposition, the royal accommodation was finally ready and was used again by the King. The result was this queasy twentieth-century neoclassical villa, stiff and substantial in the centre, but its wings papery and perforated by loggias. During the dictatorship it was used as one of the residences of the President of the Republic, and it is now the Museum of Decorative Arts. This may change when the music finally stops in the game of musical chairs in which all Barcelona's museums were engaged in 1991. The gardens were rearranged in geometrical style in 1925, and again in 1983 when the **Font Gaudí** which had previously adorned Güell's garden was re-erected in the bamboo grove in the front of the palace to the west. It is in the form of a cast and wrought-iron dragon from whose jaws water dribbles into a small stone bath.

Moderne to modern

139G **Col·legi Públic *Ramon Llull* (school)** 1919–23
Avinguda Diagonal, 269-275
Josep Goday i Casals
M Sagrada Família

Two wings of four storeys are arranged on either
side of a small entrance pavilion to form a small
palace facing the avenue. The shaky architecture
(*two* attics) is decorated with horizontal mouldings
and in *esgrafiats* in tea-set colours of green, cream
and brown. See also Goday's contemporary schools
Baixeras **136**, *Milà i Fontanals* **137** and *Pere Vila*
140, and the later *Collasso i Gil* **158** of 1932.

140 Jd **Col·legi Públic *Pere Vila* (school)** 1920–30
Avinguda de Lluís Companys, 24
Josep Goday i Casals
M Arc de Triomf

Of the five Goday schools listed here, this has the
most ample site, allowing the accommodation to
be separated into two large wings which are
symmetrically disposed to enclose the front yard.
For decoration Goday used his *noucentista* palette
of thin architectural elements in terracotta and
between them *esgrafiat* panels by Francesc
Canyelles. See also Goday's contemporary schools
Baixeras **136**, *Milà i Fontanals* **137**, and *Ramon Llull*
139, and the later *Collasso i Gil* **158** of 1932.

141F **Casa Planells** 1923–24
Avinguda Diagonal, 332/carrer de Sicília
Josep Maria Jujol i Gilbert
M Glories

Jujol, an assistant of one of Gaudí and twenty-seven
years his junior, carried out much of the brilliant
decorative work on the Casa Batlló **118**, Casa Milà **119**
and Park Güell **100**. His first independently credited
work, this is perhaps the first building in Barcelona to
suggest the difference between *Modernisme* and
modern architecture. But Jujol's *oeuvre* is so idiosyncratic that this may be accidental. The plainness of the
upper parts may be as much the result of expediency
as of artistic intention: the first project was eclectic
baroque. From a stone base with primitive cave-like
openings, rise four floors of maisonettes: each dwelling is on two floors. While their plans are as rectangular as the polygonal site will allow, the face to
avinguda Diagonal is adorned with two bulbous
cantilevered balconies which flank a vertically continuous bay window, and one of which smooths the
building round the acute angle.

142F Cine Coliseo 1923

Gran Via de les Corts Catalanes, 595

Francesc de Pau Nebot i Torrens

M Catalunya

While the Teatro Tívoli **134** was converted to a cinema shortly after it opened, the Cine Coliseo was Barcelona's first purpose-built cinema. Its huge façade to the Gran Via displays the importance of the new entertainment form but seems stranded between grandeur and grandiloquence. It contains every element of a Borromini church: towers, arches, bulging bays and, set back, a dome, but all mediated through the nineteenth-century French academy.

143I Palaus de Alfonso XIII y de Victoria Eugenia 1923–28

Plaça del Marquès de Foronda, Montjuïc

Josep Puig i Cadafalch

M Espanya

These two huge exhibition halls were built and then used for what, after many delays, eventually became Barcelona's International Exposition of 1929. Their exteriors are a stark demonstration of Puig's standard method of design : the intensely wrought eclectic porches are placed against vast flat walls, featureless except for the now-faded *esgrafiats*. But although they appear cheaply built, the halls have stood for sixty years. The little 'Turkish' kiosks which mark the rooflines at the corners corners have achieved immortality by appearing in the background of the standard photographs of Mies' pavilion **151**.

Moderne to modern

144Jb **Plaça de Catalunya** 1925–27

Francesc de Pau Nebot i Torrens, Pere Domènech i Roura, Antoni Darder, Fèlix Azúa, Enric Català i Català

M Catalunya

The plaça has always occupied an important site in Barcelona's urban development. While the city was still confined within its walls, the site was an open and public field used for recreation and assemblies. Cerdà planned to monumentalise the square as the junction between the Gran Via, the northern start of the Ramblas, and the southern end of the passeig de Gràcia. His plan was never realised, and development was carried out piecemeal, without an overall architectural scheme, but the present swirling traffic is much as he had intended. As part of the sprucing-up of the city in preparation for the International Exposition of 1929, the plaça was landscaped in the form of a circular feature with paving, walls and gateposts. The two large circular fountains were designed by Josep Maria Jujol i Gilbert and finished in 1928. In 1991 the western side, which is lined with the only buildings which date from the plaça's original setting-out, was excavated to make an underground car park, its roof landscaped with a tree-lined pedestrian reservation. This connects the Ramblas and the Rambla de Catalunya to the north and forms a continuous ribbon of trees from the sea to avinguda Diagonal.

145I **Poble Espanyol (Spanish Village)** 1927–29

Avinguda del Marqués de Comillas

Francesc Folgera i Grassi, Ramon Reventós i Farrarons, Miquel Utrillo i Morlius and Xavier Nogués i Cases

M Espanya

The Village was built to be a popular attraction contrasting with the more gritty industrial content of the 1929 Exposition. It presents a zoo of Spanish building types from all periods, parts of Spain, and of all styles, loosely strung together on terraces cut out of the side of Montjuïc. While the serpentine form is similar to that of Mies van der Rohe's layout for the Weissenhof Siedlung at Stuttgart of 1927, the picturesque urbanistic techniques are derived from those of Camillo Sitte. The individual buildings are well made, but the total effect is indigestible, and the Village's present use as a theme park has reduced their original scholarly correctness to kitsch.

146F **Myrurgia cosmetics factory** 1928–30
Carrer de Mallorca, 351/carrer Napols
Antoni Puig i Gairalt

M Verdaguer

This is one of the earliest examples in Barcelona of the *moderne* architecture strongly influenced by contemporary Parisian fashion (launched at the Exposition des Arts Decoratifs in 1925). The factory buildings with strip windows occupy the northern part of the site on one edge of the block, while the entrance to the administration's offices is marked on the corner by an artistic frontispiece with a sculptured frieze.

147I **Flats** 1928
Carrer de Lleida, 9-11
Ramon Reventós

M Espanya/Poble sec

A residential example of the early arrival in Barcelona of the Parisian-derived *moderne* architecture, the chief modelling of the symmetrical façade is produced by bringing the stairs on to the front of the building and then projecting their triangular landings. In the earlier flat types of the *Eixample* the stairs had always been embedded in the centre of the plan. Above the traditional grey granite plinth are the four storeys of flats, their windows with horizontal subdivisions, the horizontality repeated in the residual string courses in the pink stucco. The two-storey attic is of brick. There is another smaller block of three bays round the corner in carrer Tamarit.

Moderne to modern

148I Font Màgica (illuminated fountains) 1929
Avinguda de la Reina Maria Cristina, Montjuïc
Carles Buïgas, engineer

M Espanya

Puig i Cadafalch laid out the avenue and terraces
connecting the plaça Espanya to the Palau Nacional.
The gently sloping first section was decorated with
these fountains whose electric lighting in changing
colours celebrated the original theme of the exhibition and the Rivera regime. The axis culminated
in the circular pool and fountain which were also
illuminated, and the ensemble still provides one of
Barcelona's postcard archetypes. The avenue was
re-landscaped in 1985, architect Lluís Cantelops,
but the fountains were not fully repaired.

149I Palau Nacional now **Museu d'Art Catalunya**
1929
Mirador del Palau, Montjuïc
*Pere Domènech i Roura, P.E. Cendoya i Oscoz,
Enric Català i Català*

M Espanya

At the time of writing the building is being reconstructed and the contents of the museum re-
ordered. Occupying one of the prominences on the
mountain of Montjuïc, the Palau was planned as the
centrepiece of the 1929 International Exposition
and to terminate the monumental axis originally
proposed by Puig i Cadafalch. The axis, now the
avinguda de la Reina Maria Cristina, starts at the
Plaça d'Espanya to the north. A competition was
held for the design which all the prominent local
architects entered. But although the winner Pere
Domènech was Domènech i Montaner's son, who
while working on this building was still finishing the
Hospital of Sant Pau **106** started by his father, there
is no hint of *Modernisme* here. Instead, and after
the organisational and cultural muddles which
characterised the planning of the Exposition, grandiose Spanish national values are celebrated in a
brutal amalgam of Roman and Spanish Classicism
whose composition culminates in the enormous
elliptical central space with ceiling paintings by
Francesc Galí.

150| Palau de l'Agricultura now **Mercat de los Flors 1929**

Carrer de Lleida (south end, east side), Montjuïc

Manuel Mayol

Ⓜ Poble sec

Now the home of an avant-garde theatre company, this pavilion was one of the many erected for the 1929 Exposition. The plain exhibition hall faces the carrer de Lleida, while the more elaborate entrance building with its loggia and cupola is reached via an arch from a yard. The residual styling of the building is, like many of those constructed for the Exposition, in what now looks like a Hollywood version of Spanish architecture carried out in stucco with terracotta trim. Nearby in passeig de

Santa Madrona is the former **Palau de les Arts Gràfiques** by Raimon Duran Reynals, also constructed in 1929 for the Exposition but now the well-arranged **Museu Arqueologia**.

151| Pavelló Alemany (German Pavilion) **International Exhibition** 1929, 1986

Avinguda Marquès de Comillas, Montjuïc

Ludwig Mies van der Rohe; reconstruction Cristian Cirici, Fernando Ramos and Ignasi de Solà-Morales

Ⓜ Espanya

The original pavilion terminated the western end of long axis of the large plaça at the foot of the approach to the Palau Nacional but its replacement is now obscured by the unsatisfactory concrete bunker of the Olympic administration. It served as the Weimar Republic's 'hospitality suite' at the Exposition where Germany was also represented by several other buildings and exhibition sections, since demolished, that were also designed by Mies van der Rohe and Lily Reich. Mies's brief from the German government was to provide a building which would represent it as modern, forward-

looking and peaceful. Many historians now regard the Pavilion as Mies's finest building, the one in which his decade of experiments in the increasingly free manipulation of space defined by luxurious and finely-crafted materials reached its culmination. It remains one of the most important and beautiful buildings of the twentieth century.

In 1955 Barcelona architect Oriol Bohigas first formally proposed rebuilding it. In 1981 Bohigas was appointed Head of Planning Services to the Ajuntament and was able to implement the rebuilding. The work by Cirici, Ramos and Solà-Morales was well done, and only a few small and tactful changes from the original design were required to turn what was originally intended as a temporary building into a permanent one. It is now the base for a study centre: the Fundació pública del Pavelló Alemany de Barcelona de Mies van der Rohe. Postcards and documentation can be bought from its shop under the smaller of the two roofs.

Moderne to modern

152 Jc **Casal de Sant Jordi (flats)** 1929–31
Carrer de Pau Claris, 81/carrer de Casp, 24-26
Francesc Folgera i Grassi

M Urquinaona

The various functions of the building are demon-
strated in the different patterns of windows. This is
an inherently Modern proposal but it provides a
Classical composition of base, middle and top
which makes for a successful design of the twentieth century for a site on a splayed corners of the
nineteenth-century *Eixample*. Only the height suggests a dissatisfaction with the scale of the surroundings. Above the two-storey base clad in stone
are three storeys of offices and three of flats
finished in render painted slate green. The top or
cornice is provided by the owner's flat whose main
rooms face inward over a balcony to the open
space at the centre of the block, presenting only
the servants' bedroom windows to the street.

153B **Casa Vilaró *(Casa de la Barca)*** 1929
Avinguda del Coll del Portell, 43
Sixt Yllescas i Mirosa

M Lesseps

It was Sert's assistant Yllescas who first brought
the international modern style to Barcelona. From
below, all that can be seen of this large and
important house, now almost completely hidden
behind dense planting, is a blur of white-painted
rendering and a glimpse of the balconies' authen-
tically modern ship's handrails. Entered at the
upper level of its steeply sloping site, it presents a
modest single-storey wall to the street.

154F **Blanquerna School** now **Institute Menéndez
Pelayo** 1930–33
Via Augusta, 140
Jaume Maistres Fossas

F Muntaner

Painted pink and with new aluminium windows, little
of what original photographs show to have been
the original sharp modern spirit of this large school
now remains.

155E Flats 1930

Carrer del Rosselló, 36

Josep Lluís Sert i López

Ⓜ Entença

Sixt Yllescas's Casa Vilaró **153** of the previous year first brought international modern architecture to Barcelona to serve its wealthy. Sert here first provided it for humbler users. The design on the narrow plot does not use a modern 'type', but employs the traditional light and ventilation wells of domestic planning in the *Eixample*. The treatment of the balconies is, however, not traditional: they do not project and are not glazed but are paired, recessed and open.

156F Flats 1930–31

Carrer Muntaner, 342-348

Josep Lluís Sert i López and Sixt Yllescas

Ⓕ Muntaner

A much more ambitious design than the flats in carrer del Rosselló **155** of the previous year, and on a corner site in a smart district, this building shows Sert's first knowing and confident handling of those forms of modern architecture developed, for example, by Le Corbusier. The birdsmouth corner with its token cantilevered balconies which disrupt the symmetry of the front is handled with particular assurance. Each dwelling is arranged on two floors and the scale of the elevations reflects this, although the elements which supply the important modelling, the recessed horizontal slots of the balconies, are in fact outside the bedrooms rather than the living rooms. Many of Barcelona's modern buildings were painted in colour and this one is now painted pale green, as it was originally. This is still a surprise for those who assumed that buildings of the so-called International Style were a uniform white, a misunderstanding fostered by the absence in the 1930s of ubiquitous colour photography. See also for example Rodriguez Arias's flats **157** in the via Augusta.

Moderne to modern

157F   Flats 1931
Via Augusta, 61
Germán Rodriguez Arias

F Gràcia

A cheerful modern work, its rendering restored and magnificently painted in bright pink, its metalwork a jarring pale green. In a reverse of tradition its balconies are on the front of the block and are angled southwards. Many of Barcelona's modern buildings were built on sites between the party walls of existing buildings, and this allowed. as here, the language of modern architecture to be considered and displayed with as much brio as that displayed by the architects of *Modernisme* a generation earlier. See also Arias's flats and Astoria cinema of 1933–34 **161**.

158Je   Col·legi Públic *Collasso i Gil* 1932
Carrer de Sant Pau, 101
Josep Goday i Casals

M Paral·lel

The last school designed by the prolific Goday, its uncharacteristic style is the result of his visiting Scandinavia. It has the tight planning of the earlier schools and the equally cramped site of some of them. But the styling, although conservative, is entirely Swedish, and is carried out in finely crafted brickwork instead of stucco. The grand entrance set back behind its yard shows that it is a public building, but its imagery now disturbingly suggests a cinema or swimming pool rather than a school.

159D **Casa Bloc** 1932–36
Avinguda de Torres i Bages, 91-105
GATCPAC

Ⓜ Sant Andreu/Torras i Bages

This is the most important public housing scheme of the 1930s in Barcelona and one of the more significant in Europe. It was the built result of the theorising and research carried out by the group of Catalan architects GATCPAC, the Grup d'Artistes i Tècnics Catalans per al Progrés de l'Arquitectura Contemporània, which flourished in Barcelona's most Republican period in the years leading up to the Civil War. It was intended as an urban and social paradigm, and as a development from the models of freestanding 'island' housing. Occupying an area equivalent to about two *Eixample* blocks the dwellings are arranged in a continuous strip bent into an S-shape. (The open side of the S facing avinguda de Torres i Bages was filled in shortly after the building was completed.) A school occupied one of the two open spaces; the other was left as a park. The strip is made of maisonettes stacked three deep and raised off the ground on the *pilotis* of the regular steel framed structure, and each dwelling is reached from a gallery which is served by stairs at the corners. The dwellings are generously and rationally planned with the living room and large terrace on the lower floor and the bedrooms above. The details of architectural style are as sophisticatedly handled as those of any of its contemporaries: note for example how the irregular section of the flats is contained by the plain rectangular walls at the ends.

After its completion and with the outbreak of war, the building was taken over by the army and it was never occupied by the families it was originally intended to house. Restoration of the block was started in 1991, and the shops which usefully occupied the street frontage are being removed to restore the views from the surrounding streets into the internal courts.

Moderne to modern

160G **Flats** 1933
Avinguda de Gaudí, 56
Pere Benavent
Ⓜ Hospital Sant Pau

Benavent's routinely planned block is carried out in a style clearly influenced by modern developments: while the paired central balconies are similar to those of Sert's flats at carrer del Rosselló **155**, the choice of brick as facing material suggests either the influence of contemporary Amsterdam, or a continuation of the *modernista* associations of brick with Catalan identity.

161F **Flats and Astoria cinema** 1933–34
Carrer París, 193-199
Germán Rodriguez Arias
Ⓜ Diagonal

The six floors of flats are set against the standard five of the *Eixample*, and the modelling is restricted to the recesses for the projecting balconies. The cinema below has a double height foyer. While the effect is more *moderne* than modern, Arias was a member of GATCPAC and presumably more serious than the cheerful results here suggest. The pale green paint was, or later became, the standard livery for many of Barcelona's modern and *moderne* buildings. See also Arias' earlier flats of 1931 in the via Augusta **157**.

162F Flats 1934
Carrer d'Aribau, 243/camp d'en Vidal, 16
Raimon Duran Reynals

F Sant Gervasi

Modern architecture for Barcelona's working class
was first introduced by Sert: see his flats of 1930
at Carrer del Rosselló, 36 **155**. Here is the first
example for the bourgeoisie, a expansively large
block simply proportioned and well detailed. It lies
between two streets and the front is to the smaller
of the two, camp d'en Vidal, and is topped with an
elegant but un-modern flat cornice.

Façade to carrer d'Aribau

163J Joieria *Roca* (jewellery shop) 1934
Passeig de Gràcia, 18
Josep Lluís Sert i López

M Passeig de Gràcia

While hardly germane to the social programme of
modern architecture, shop design often provided
the opportunity for virtuoso displays of the possi-
bilities of the style. Here is a well preserved
exercise in horizontal composition and in the elegant use of materials: orange-grey granite, clear
glass display windows, a clerestory of modern
architecture's very own glass blocks, all these set
in a narrow frame of black granite.

164 Jb **Dispensari Central Antituberculós** 1934–38

Carrer de Torres i Amat/passeig de Sant Bernat, 10

Josep Lluís Sert i López, J. Torres i Clavé and Joan B. Subirana i Subirana

M Universitat

Casa Bloc **159** and this dispensary are the two flagships of modern architecture in Barcelona. Both demonstrate the connection between the style and the social programme with which its GATCPAC architects wished to be associated, and which they expected the style would help bring into being. It was the last building on which all three architects worked before the Civil War separated them, and before Sert left for the USA.

In what may be either a conscious or unconscious reference to Mediterranean tradition, the accommodation is arranged in blocks distinguished by function around an entrance courtyard planted with trees which provide shade. To the left of the gate, the main wing housed three storeys of consulting rooms which are lifted off the ground and supported on *pilotis*. The symmetrically-organised block at the end of the courtyard contained a lecture room on the top floor. Both the planning and the style show an astonishingly refined understanding of late modern architecture subtly moderated by local usages and conditions. The building is probably only less well known than it deserves to be because it was completed after the first publi-

cation of Hitchcock and Johnson's book *International Style* of 1932. While originally embedded in its surrounding streets, in the ambitious re-building of the Caritat district the refurbished building will acquire a new and monumental setting.

165B **Flats** 1934

Carrer de Pàdua, 96

Sixt Yllescas i Mirosa

F Pàdua

Yllescas, architect of the suburban and luxurious casa Vilaró of 1929 **153**, here gave a neat and considered modern treatment to Barcelona's characteristic urban format of five residential floors on a ground floor for commerce. While all the original work remains, including the delicate ironwork to the cantilevered balconies and the bronze entrance door, a thorough restoration would reveal the block's elegance.

166F **Clínica Barraquer, Centro de Oftalmología** 1936–39

Carrer de Muntaner, 314/carrer Laforja

Joaquim Lloret i Homs

F Muntaner

Commissioned by a Doctor Barraquer, the building's various functions are zoned by floor, with consulting rooms at ground level, rooms for patients on the first floor, with five floors of flats above these. The top floor provided a penthouse for the doctor. Stainless steel pilasters and the glazed landings of the projecting staircase unite these layers. The planning and style are a world away from the 'progressive' modernism of Sert and his colleagues, and owe much to contemporary German and American commercial architecture, with a flavour of Art Deco in the details.

Moderne to modern

167 Jc **Gratacels Urquinaona** 1936–42

Carrer de les Jonqueres, 18/carrer de Trafalgar

Project: Luis Gutiérrez Soto; execution: Carles Martinez i Sánchez

M Urquinaona

When it was built this block of flats of fifteen stories was the tallest occupied building in Barcelona. (The towers of Sagrada Família are higher.) In a conservative and oppressive modern style, it could either be welcomed as a useful counterpoint to the monotony of the *Eixample* or as an absurd and unnecessary effort by an architect from Madrid merely to upset its uniformity.

168Jb Banc Vitalici de Espanya 1942–50

Passeig de Gràcia, 11/Gran via de les Corts Catalanes, 632

Lluís Bonet i Garí

Ⓜ Catalunya

Of the very few buildings of the 1940s in the city, only the monumental buildings for financial institutions which clutter the streets around plaça de Catalunya record the early years of the Francoist era. All ignore earlier ordinances about height and bulk in the *Eixample*, and all are in a weary neoclassical style which lacked either the verve or the correctness of contemporary commercial building in the United States. The only original idea which their architects brought to the programme was the crowning square tower set where possible on the splayed corner of a Cerdà blocks. This bank is one of the least offensive of this bombastic genre.

169J Flats for ISM employees 1952–54

Passeig Nacional, 43/carrer Almirall Cervera

José Antonio Coderch de Sentmenat and Manuel Valls i Vergés

Ⓜ Barceloneta

ISM was the fishermen's pension fund which commissioned these flats. When completed they were regarded as one of the first signs of a revival in Catalan architecture following Spain's cultural and economic stagnation since 1936. But it is now possible to see that the 'organic' features of the building were influenced as much by contemporary Italian work as by local tradition. There are two flats on each floor. Their rooms are trapezoidal, and their shapes project on to the exterior giving the very slight angled inflections. The general crispness of the facade, with its alternating bands of ochre tiles and panels of screened windows, characterises much of Coderch's later work.

The Franco era

170F *Escorial* **residential area** 1952–62

Carrer de l'Escorial, 50/carrer de la Legalitat

Josep M Ribas i Casas and Francesc Mitjans i Miró, Josep Soteras i Mauri

M Joanic

Most cities in the world have at least one of these progressive developments derived from CIAM's recipes, and this was Barcelona's first. It uses the vertical rather than the horizontal model of Casa Bloc **159**. The earlier buildings are at the southwest corner of the block: a seventeen-storey residential slab,its lift and stairs fashionably detached. A separate commercial building of two storeys is set at right angles to the street. The lower slabs to the north at the edges of the block are later. *Escorial* enjoys the benefits and disadvantages of all such developments. All the flats have plentiful light and air, much of the ground is free of building, and considerable areas are protected from traffic. But shops and offices which ordinarily line the pavement are drawn back into the site, and the means of access to the flats becomes indirect. The liberated space remains semi-private and has no conventional function, and the benefits are bought at the expense of the city as a whole whose comprehensible and ordinary pattern of streets becomes disrupted.

171E **Campo del fútbol, Club Barcelona** 1954–57

Travessera de les Corts/avinguda del Papa XXIII

Lorenzo Garcia Barbón and Francesc Mitjans i Miró etc

M Collblanc

Formerly stranded on its dusty suburban site, work on the stadium to integrate it more into its setting was undertaken for the 1992 Olympic Games.

From the outside the concrete structure is lumpy and the detailing crude, and the only spirited forms are the two pedestrian ramps on the western side. But for one of Europe's foremost and successful football clubs it is the interior which is more important, and here 120,000 spectators can be accommodated in three continuous tiers planned in a standard modern snubbed oval. The Club's administration is housed in the nearby antique farmhouse, the Masia can Planas **29**.

172E Editorial Gustavo Gili 1954–61

Carrer del Rosselló, 89

Francesc Bassó i Birulés and Joaquim Gill i Moros

M Entença

The arrangement of this headquarters for the Gili publishing group presents a challenge to the more orthodox development of a single *Eixample* block. Here the whole of the *inside* of the block, usually inaccessible from the street and used for workshops or gardens, is developed as a large landscaped campus reached by a gated entrance from the street. The experiment is not entirely successful: the original glamour of the low modern build- ings has now faded, the landscaping is not lavish enough, and too much of the ground seems devoted to vehicles.

173E Flats 1957–61

Carrer de Johann Sebastian Bach, 7

José Antonio Coderch de Sentmenat and Manuel Valls i Vergés

F Bonanova

The whole north side of the street has been developed with a regular series of blocks of flats of six storeys. This block is one of the most distinguished, its effects precisely calculated. Coderch had used blinds to make part of the surface of his earlier ISM flats **169**, but here the whole street façade is covered in adjustable aluminium blinds separated by thin stone string courses and enclosed at the ends by panels of pink brickwork. The only modelling is supplied by the projecting triangular balconies which are also partly screened.

See also, nearby, Taller Bofill's flats at Carrer de Johann Sebastian Bach, 28,**180**; and Coderch's housing at carrer de Raset, **195**.

174A Facultat de Dret (Law Faculty) 1958

Avinguda Diagonal, 684, Pedralbes

Guillermo Giràldez Dávila, Pedro López Iñigo and Xavier Subias i Fages

M Palau Reial

In 1958 a new university campus was established at the western end of avinguda Diagonal and the Law Faculty was among the first of the new buildings. When completed it was highly regarded for its challenge to the prevailing dull neoclassicism with which institutions had generally been clothed. But both the composition, a 'dynamic' contrast of vertical tower and horizontal podium, and the language, an unspecific international modernism, now look dull, and many of the details were insufficiently robust to retain the crispness which the language demanded.

The Franco era

175Jf Col·legi d'Arquitectes de Catalunya 1958–62
Plaça Nova, 5
Xavier Busquets i Sindreu

M Jaume I

The College of Architects is presumably now slightly embarrassed by this extremely dated affair, but it was the result of a competition. The only alternative to demolition is to wait in the hope that the buildings of this period become appreciated again. The decorative *esgrafiat* frieze on the podium on which the tower sits is from a design by Picasso. Meanwhile, the shop front to the pavement provides a view of the constantly changing exhibitions about current architecture which the College enterprisingly and regularly mounts, and in the basement there is an excellent architectural bookshop and a shop for drawing office supplies.

176G Flats 1959–62
Carrer Padilla, 323-327
Antoni de Moragas i Gallissà and Francesc de Riba i Salas

M Hospital Sant Pau

An undistinguished but very early example in what was to become Moragas and de Riba's programme of experimentation in the style and organisation of blocks of flats. Their early attachment to Brutalism is evident in the aggressive plant troughs in front of the living room windows. The grey mosaic panels are internationally drab rather than locally cheerful.

177Jb Offices for Hispano-Olivetti 1960–64
Ronda de la Universitat, 18
Project: Ludovico Belgiojoso/BBPR; execution: Josep Soteras i Mauri

M Catalunya

The international programme launched by Adriano Olivetti to provide showrooms and offices for the company regularly employed distinguished local architects, but here the distinction was imported from Milan. The block contributes to the repertoire of plans for office buildings in having a central row of paired columns from which the floors span on to the party walls on either side. The aluminium curtain wall whose stepping in plan hints at the building's central organisation was the first such façade in Barcelona, but it has now weathered to an unpleasant ochre colour.

178H Flats 1960–65

Avinguda de la Meridiana, 312-314

Josep M. Martorell i Codina, Oriol Bohigas Guardiola, David Mackay Goodchild

M Sagrera

Sited at an inflection of one of Europe's most terrifying roads, the avinguda de la Meridiana, which here is twelve lanes wide, this block of 121 flats stands out from the banality of its neighbours: it aspires to architecture. The dimensions of the block were determined by planners, but its organisation shows considerable ingenuity. Two rows of flats are separated by an open strip which provides ventilation to their backs and which houses the elements of vertical circulation. Conforming to Barcelona convention, and avoiding *pilotis*, the flats ride above a ground floor of shops on a delicately vaulted platform. The style, like that of many of Martorell Bohigas and Mackay's earlier buildings, owes much to contemporary Italian work. The façade, lacking any obviously tectonic elements, is instead composed of a texture of repeated small oriel windows alternating with panels of orange tile. The randomness with which these are placed is the consequence of the complex arrangement of flats of different sizes, and was perhaps intended to reduce the apparent bulk of the block. But the effect if any is denied by the aggressive and coarsely detailed mansard which crowns the building.

179G Flats 1960–62

Carrer Navas de Tolosa, 296

Josep M. Martorell i Codina, Oriol Bohigas Guardiola, David Mackay Goodchild

M Navas

A seven-storey block of flats over a ground floor of shops. The continuous verticals allow the block easily to negotiate its chamfered corner, but no more elegantly than some of the more ordinary examples of the *Eixample*, and the over-use of the forty-five degree geometry now seems mannered. The use of red brick and yellow glazed slip tiles demonstrates the practice's concern to enrich the conventional language of modern architecture by

developing extensions of it including local motifs and materials, particularly the traditional ceramic products of Catalonia.

The Franco era

180F **Flats** 1960–62

Carrer Johann Sebastian Bach, 28

Taller d'Arquitectura Bofill

F Bonanova

A small and very modest block of flats from the earliest years of the practice, its architecture made up of the sliding screens across the windows. See also the Taller's later block at the other end of carrer Johann Sebastian Bach, 4.

181G **Flats** 1961–64

Ronda del Guinardó/carrer de Lepant, 42-44

Josep M. Martorell i Codina, Oriol Bohigas Guardiola, David Mackay Goodchild

M Alfons X

Two blocks face each other across the corners of the carrer de Lepant, and their composition demonstrates the practice's first involvement with then current Brutalist forms. The brick is 'poor' and it is combined with raw concrete and skimpy window frames, and the composition is small-scaled and emphasises the particular elements.

Note immediately to the north on the other side of ronda del Guinardó the little 'Moorish' pavilion handsomely refurbished in 1989 to house the Ajuntament's Horta-Guinardó district offices.

182F

Casa Tàpies 1962–63

Carrer de Saragossa, 57

José Antonio Coderch de Sentmenat

F Plaça Molina

In a quiet street, a discreet studio house of three storeys for the artist Tàpies presents a chaste and skinny white-painted steel frame filled with narrow panels of the architect's favourite louvres. Both the form and colour of the architectural proposal are in marked opposition to the exuberant shagginess and occasional violence of the client's work now exhibited in his Fundació **70**.

183E

Schenkel flats 1962–64

Carrer del marqués de Sentmenat, 68/carrer de Nicaragua, 99

Taller d'Arquitectura Bofill

M Sants Estació

A virtuoso effort in getting round an oblique corner, the flats appear to consist of a slew of vertical and windowless brick planes, some with horizontal slits and with balconies at their ends. The main windows are set back behind the edges of the planes and are turned to catch as much sun as the north-facing site permits. The broken-up roofscape is enlivened with chimneys and ventilators whose forms are derived from Gaudí's.

See also the Taller's contemporary work at carrer Johann Sebastian Bach, 2 and 28 **180**.

The Franco era

184A Madre Guell Convent 1963–67
Carrer Esperança, 5-7
Lluís Cantelops and J. Rodrigo Dalmau

F Reina Elisenda

One of the small stock of Barcelona's brutalist buildings, the residential block is built of finely crafted and sensitively composed impoverished brickwork and raw concrete. The style always was more appropriate to some uses than others, and the appropriate included religious institutions.

185Je Flats 1963
Ronda Sant Pau, 42-44
Antoni de Moragas i Gallissà and Francesc de Riba i Salas

M Sant Antoni

A large and fussy contribution to the street scene which doubles the scale of buildings along the ronda. It draws attention to its conventional functions with timid modelling achieved by setting the structure parallel to the party walls rather than the street and then showing the cantilevered beam ends. The green ceramic spandrel panels are a nod to local tradition.

186F *El Noticiero Universal* workshop and offices 1963–65
Carrer de Roger de Llúria, 35
Josep Maria Sostres i Maluquer

M Passeig de Gràcia

An extension to the newspaper offices housed in the building on the corner to the north, this small block is mentioned only because it was thought noteworthy among the generally unremarkable work of the 1960s in Barcelona. Its flush, poorly proportioned façade of precast panels which, when new, could be seen as heroic and revolutionary, now demonstrates that modern architecture required just as much care as any other kind, and that abstraction or omission in themselves could guarantee neither immediate success nor lasting cultural significance.

187E **Flats** 1964–66

Carrer Entença, 99

Josep M. Martorell i Codina, Oriol Bohigas Guardiola, David Mackay Goodchild

M Tarragona

In an ambitious attempt to find an alternative to the *Eixample*'s standard pattern of development which follows the street frontage, two residential towers with irregular plans are set back from the street and placed above a continuous floor of commercial uses. While each building is topped with a small yellow-tiled mansard of the kind since popularised by McDonalds, the styling generally follows mannered contemporary Italian work, but the aluminium

window frames have not weathered gracefully. Note also the spirited modern block of flats to the south at carrer Entença, 95.

188F **Banca Catalana** 1965–68

Passeig de Gràcia, 84

Josep Maria Fargas i Falp and Enric Tous i Carbó

M Diagonal

The design of this large commercial building was the result of an architectural competition held among Catalan architects. Although the winner's façade to passeig de Gràcia must have seemed like a good idea at the time, the years have been unkind both to the estimation of the small collection of clichés with which it is composed and to its would-be ritzy material, the profiled copper-coloured anodised aluminium panels. While its surface offers no particular pleasure, the building's virtue is that it does not disrupt the pattern of the street as much as it might have done.

189E *Trade* **offices** 1966-69

Avinguda Gran Via de Carles III, 86-94

José Antonio Coderch de Sentmenat and Manuel Valls i Vergés

M Maria Cristina

In the establishment in the 1960s of a new commercial centre to the north-west and well outside the city's earlier boundaries, these four stumpy towers were among the first buildings. Their scale is appropriate to their location, facing what was to become one of the city's three main ring roads. The blocks' enigmatically undulating sealed surfaces of sombre curtain walling are perhaps a response both to the irregularity of their site and to the vagueness of the brief. For Coderch, the language was completely new: the masonry, frames and louvres of his earlier domestic architecture are absent.

The Franco era

190F **Flats** 1966–68

Carrer de Brusi, 39-43/via Augusta, 128-132

Antoni de Moragas i Gallissà and Francesc de Riba i Salas

F Sant Gervasi

The block shows the architects continuing their exploration of housing types in the otherwise exhausted architectural debate in the Spain of the time. This is one of the most spirited and controlled examples of their particular brand of Brutalism applied to an otherwise routine programme of six storeys of flats above two of shops. Brutalism's projecting concrete beam ends, originally launched by Le Corbusier's Maisons Jaoul, are here wittily used to support the planting boxes in front of the living-room windows, and are combined with appropriate local materials of brick and tile. The modelling approaches, however timidly, that of the more full blooded Modernista blocks in the *Eixample*.

See also the same architects' earlier work, the flats at carrer Padilla **176** and on the ronda Sant Pau, 42-44 **185**.

191F *Atalaya* **offices and flats** 1967–71

Avinguda Diagonal, 523/avinguda de Sarrià, 71

Frederic Correa i Ruiz and Alfonso Milà i Sagnier, José Luis Sanz Magallón

F Muntaner

When built this was the tallest occupied building in Barcelona, and its erection contributed to the establishment of the commercial zone then being developed along the north west end of avinguda Diagonal. Its very particular profile results from its zoning: there are offices on the lower floors and flats of two different types above; and from the organisation of its plan which is formed by the symmetry of rotation around the lifts and stairs in the centre. The glazing of the projecting restaurant at the top provides a broken cornice. The obsessive white cladding of U-shaped precast concrete panels was clearly influenced by the work of the contemporary Italian avant-garde.

92A Flats 1967

Carrer de Dr Carulla, 53

Josep M. Martorell i Codina, Oriol Bohigas Guardiola, David Mackay Goodchild

F Tres torres

The apotheosis of the architects' enchantment with the Italian neo-Liberty style, this semi-detached block of flats set in a charming suburb presents a façade of vertical panels of white stucco alternating with deliberately irregular pre-cast balconies with perforated balustrades, all topped by a McDonalds mansard.

93A *Les Escales Park* housing 1967–73

Carrer de Sor Eulàlia d'Anzizu, 38-46

Project: Sert, Jackson and Associates; execution: Estudi Anglada/Gelabert/Ribas

M Palau Reial

The building of these flats mark Sert's return to Barcelona after having been in the United States since 1938 when the Dispensari Central Anti-tuberculós **164** was finished. The single linear block, which ranges from five to eight storeys, is arranged parallel to the street and set back from it behind the now lush landscaping that this sort of architecture has always needed as complement. Closely following Sert's contemporary American work in the student housing at Cambridge, Massachusetts of the earlier nineteen-sixties, their deliberately picturesque irregular profile is provided both in plan and elevation and ordered only by the regular positioning of the stair towers. Although the language and precast concrete panels had become used internationally, some of the materials, including the panels of orange tiling, are appropriately local, as are the various devices for sun-screening and the very un-modern chimneys.

The Franco era

194F Caixa de Barcelona 1968–73
Avinguda Diagonal, 522-532/carrer de Moià, 3
Xavier Busquets i Sindreu

M Diagonal

In a drastic and radical approach to the architecture of the street, the repetitious requirements of the bank's offices are screened from the street by an elegant glazed curtain wall sheltered from the sun by movable fins of bronze glass. The ensemble effortlessly continues the cornice and building lines of the.avinguda Diagonal. The achievement is remarkable for its time: most of the technology and materials had to be imported into a then industrially backward Spain.

195F Housing 1968–74
Carrer de Raset, 21-31/carrer de Freixa, 22-32
José Antonio Coderch de Sentmenat

F Muntaner

A model of 'Mediterranean' housing for the middle classes, this scheme is expansive, well built and well landscaped, and although in a suburban setting, achieves a high density without the use of high buildings. Two rows of pavilions of four and five storeys are set parallel to the street, each pavilion having a highly serrated plan form. Coderch again followed his general rule in composing a façade with as few lines as possible, and the flats are clad entirely in continuous vertical panels of bright orange-red tiles laid vertically. Between the tilework are panels of glass and both these and the luxuriously large terraces are screened with fixed timber louvres.

196E Flats 1968

Avinguda Diagonal, 628-630

Guillermo Giràldez Dávila, Pedro López Iñigo and Xavier Subias i Fages

F Bonanova

A large housing scheme of fourteen-storey slabs as well executed as the brief and setting would allow. The earlier consensus about the form of the city has finally collapsed, and the sociable and continuous blocks of the *Eixample* have given way to the internationally-styled enclave, its individual buildings more or less well designed.

197I Fundació *Joan Miró* 1972–74 and since extended

Avinguda de Miramar, Montjuïc

Project: Sert, Jackson and Associates; execution: Estudi Anglada/Gelabert/Ribas

M Espanya

Sert returned to Barcelona in 1967 to build the flats at Carrer de Sor Eulàlia d'Anzizu **193**. The result of his friendship with the artist, this slightly later building for the Miró Foundation was his first opportunity to design an institution since the Dispensary **164** of 1938. Unlike the art of Picasso, whose early work is now housed in the museum in the heart of the Ciutat vella **8**, Miró's was seen as the object of contemplation and leisure rather than as a challenge to the city, and the Foundation was safely located on a beautiful but suburban site in Montjuïc park. Both the informing idea of the building and its style owe much to Sert's former employer and colleague Le Corbusier, but in Sert's hands the rough concrete and poetic gestures of

Le Corbusier's late work became stiffer and more academic than those of his master. Much of the originally bare concrete has subsequently been painted a blinding white, bringing the architecture dangerously close to the prettiness of a Mediterranean developer's holiday village.

The galleries for the prolific Miró's work constitute the bulk of accommodation and are wrapped around an irregular landscaped courtyard to form an 'architectural promenade' with a standard clockwise circulation. Roofed with small barrel vaults, they are lit with projecting monitors or light scoops which suggest the building's use from the outside. The monitors proved all too successful in scooping the light and are now mostly blocked up. The flat roofs of the galleries are incorporated into the promenade and provide settings for sculpture and good views to the north and west over the city. Since its completion, the building has been extended to the right of the entrance with a library and octagonal lecture room. Further extensions along the road to the east are planned.

Dancing the *sadana*, pla de la Seu, Sunday morning

Post-Franco and democracy 1975–

98A Extension to the Escuela Técnica Superior de Arquitectura de Barcelona 1978–86

Carrer Adolph Florensa

José Antonio Coderch de Sentmenat

Ⓜ Zona Universitaria

The two-storey extension provides an exhibition space and lecture and seminar rooms. Each room is articulated and surrounded by a curly wall, and the whole clad in Coderch's characteristic hard red tile, a foil to the cream and dullness of the School's earlier building. Coderch had been Professor at the School of Architecture from 1965 to 1968, and this, his last work in Barcelona, was completed after his death in 1984.

99E Plaça del Països Catalans 1981–83

Sants Estació

Helio Piñon i Pallarés and Alberto Viaplana i Vea with Enric Miralles i Moya

Ⓜ Sants-Estació

The station at Sants had escaped the under–grounding of the railway lines which had been proposed in Cerdà's far-sighted transport plan. In the late 1970s, however, the station was redeveloped and the lines put into a tunnel, leaving only the new neat but undistinguished single-storey shed facing the varied and unpromising surroundings to its east and west. This site became the location for one of the first and largest 'parks' of the programme launched in the 1980s (see Introduction). Piñon and Viaplana's proposal was one of the first to draw the world's attention to the extraordinary explosion of Spanish and Catalan cultural energy which followed the end of the Francoist period in 1975. The two main features are the linear canopy with its serpentine roof which launches itself at the station from both sides, and the 15-metre high square structure on the east side. Both are roofed in open expanded metal mesh, and so perhaps ironically neither offers shelter from the rain. These and the various subsidiary structures are placed on the subtly articulated and decorated granite-covered ground plane and are carried out in an enigmatic abstract style, much of whose meaning remains elusive. While the scheme certainly succeeds in overcoming its tatty surroundings, offering a potent image to those who may be capable of reading it, it has suffered from the general faults of many of the other parks in the programme: since most of the fittings were specially designed, they are neither maintained nor repaired. The author has yet to see the ingenious fountains working.

Post-Franco and democracy

200H Plaça de la Palmera 1981–83

Carrer d'Andrade/carrer de Maresme/carrer del Concili de Trento

Richard Serra and Ajuntament de Barcelona, Servei de Projectes i Elements Urbans

M Besós/La Pau

The first park to be set in a district of workers' housing offered something for everybody. The 'popular' elements, bandstand and trees are to the west. Serra's curved wall, which breaks to provide a setting for the palm tree which gives the park its name, separates the popular from the more enigmatic gravelled area lit by a lighting standard of Russian Constructivist provenance. A broad, stepped and tree-lined terrace on the east side provides a setting for walking the dog and contemplating the concept. But Serra's conceptual radiating ribs which originally projected from the gravelled surface have since been removed, perhaps because people tripped over them and they prevented the space being used for football.

201F Plaça del Sol 1982–85

Plaça del Sol, Gràcia

Jaume Bach i Nuñez, Gabriel Mora i Gramunt

M Fontana

As part of a general programme to curb traffic in Gràcia, the cars which used to infest the square were placed under it and the paved roof of their shelter now provides for pedestrians and café terraces. The new architecture is concentrated on the west side where the diminutive car ramps are screened by a simple steel shelter. Three decorated lamp standards and benches on the north side and the zodiacal sundial on the east complete the furnishing. The square can now serve as a viewing platform for the varied buildings which surround it (note, for example, the block in the north east corner with pretty pink *esgrafiats* on a green ground). Bach and Mora also designed two more schemes nearby: the **Plaça Trilla**, the small squares which lie on either side of the carrer Gran de Gràcia just north of the Fontana Metro station, and the much larger **Plaça Virreina** to the east of plaça del Sol.

202E Parc de l'Espanya Industrial 1982–85

Avinguda de Roma

Project: Lluís Peña-Ganchegui; execution: with Francesc Rius i Camps

M Sants Estació

On the site of an abandoned textile factory, and its name recording this, this park is among the larger in the series. In an act of patronage characteristic of the programme it was commissioned from the Basque architect Peña-Ganchegui. It is laid it out in two zones. To the south on the site of the factory buildings, one of which is retained, is a large flat area paved with gravel and planted with shade trees. To the north is a boating lake fed by a fountain and overlooked by a stepped terrace illuminated with seven lighting towers, their look-outs now unfortunately inaccessible. The towers are decorated with the red and yellow stripes of Catalonia and Barcelona. Signalling the park's existence to its surroundings, the large and spirited dragon of Saint George in rusty sheet steel is by Barcelonan Andrés Nagel and incorporates a slide.

203B Museu de la Ciència (Science Museum)
1983

Carrer Cister/carrer Teodor Roviralta

Extension: Jordi Garcés, Enric Sòria

F Tibidabo

Originally a hospice, the older part of the building to the east was built in 1904-09 and designed by Domenech i Estapà. The conversion of the whole to a museum was carried out by Garcés and Sòria who re-ordered the interior including the new finely detailed staircase. They re-clad the exterior of the later western part of the building in abstract panels of brickwork above and to the side of the transparent entrance which now leads onto a terrace. Visible from the Museum's yard and on a promontory of the hill to the north, the striking house is the **Casa Arnús** ('El Pinar') by Enric Sagnier i Villavecchia of 1903.

Post-Franco and democracy

204C **Velòdrom d'Horta (cycling stadium)** 1984
Passeig de la Vall d'Hebron
Esteve Bonell i Costa and Francesc Rius i Camps

M Montbau

The banked oval cycle track and the spectators' seats round it are enclosed within a narrow circular ring which provides accommodation and covered entrances. Two promenades are formed by the broad spaces which remain between the back of the seats and the inside of the ring. The outer ring is capped with a slim and elegant concrete roof-plate which unites the whole composition. The building is cut into its sloping site and the entrance at the lower level gives direct access to the track, while that above is at the level of the highest specatator seats. The building presents a winning combination of breathtakingly elegant planning and a sure-handed formalism. The distant views of it from Barcelona's outer ring road are stunning, when only the jauntily angled lighting masts suggest its function. The detailing stands close inspection, but the little bridge and portal to the north on the axis of the entrance to the Laberint Horta **48** seem unnecessarily fussy. The artistic punctuation marks set in the grass are by the poet Juan Brossa.

205G **Road bridge** 1984–87
Carrer de Felipe II/carrer de Bac de Roda
Santiago Calatrava and Departamento de Projectos Urbanos, Barcelona

M Navas

The road bridge spans the main railway line that connects Barcelona with the north-east. The structure is ingenious: the road deck is suspended from *four* arches arranged in two pairs, the outer arch of each pair inclined inwards to brace its partner and connected to it at the crown. The road deck arrives at the ground at either end of the bridge via an artistically profiled concrete abutment. Lighting for both road and pavements is neatly incorporated into the balustrades.

The triangular site between carrer de Felipe II and carrer Palencia to the north of the bridge has been laid out as the **Plaça General Moragas**, another of the series of parks of the 1980s. It was designed by Olga Tarrasó of the Ajuntament's Ambit d'Urbanisme i Serveis Municipals, and features sloping surfaces which are good for skateboarding, and sculpture by Ellsworth Kelly.

206G **Parc del Clot** 1984–87

Carrer Escultors Claperos, Clot

Dani Freixes, Vincente Miranda

M Clot

On a triangular site formerly occupied by a railway factory, the park serves the inhabitants of the dense housing surrounding it. It is divided into three zones, from west to east: a gravelled area planted with trees, a large sunken pitch for ball games, and a small conventional park with grass and planted with indigenous pines and cypress trees. These zones are united and crossed by two bridges which span between the various levels. At the perimeter some remains of the factory have been preserved, and the old wall to carrer Escultors Claperos is now lined with a pool.

207J **Centre d'Art Santa Monica** 1985–89

La Rambla/carrer Santa Monica

Alberto Viaplana i Vea and Helio Piñon i Pallarés with R. Mercader

M Drassanes

The conversion of the church buildings to an art gallery gave the architects the opportunity to develop their idiosyncratic formal vocabulary after designing the more radical Plaça del Països Catalans **199**.

208E **Parc de Joan Miró** ex **Parc de l'Escorrxador** 1985

Carrer Tarragona/carrer Arragó

Antoni Solanas, Andreu Arriola, Beth Gali, Màrius Quintana

M Espanya

Occupying an area equivalent to four *Eixample* blocks and on the site of a former slaughterhouse ('escorrxador'), this park is among the more formally laid out of the programme. The geometry of the blocks is preserved: the north-west quadrant is slightly raised above street level, paved, and undecorated, providing settings for Miró's colourful erotic sculpture *Woman and Bird*, whose base stands in a pool, and for social events on public holidays. The remaining L-shape of the site is sunk below its surroundings and decorated with a dense grove of flourishing and alternating palm and pine trees in which are disposed a pergola, places to sit, tennis courts and patches of gravel for bowls.

Post-Franco and democracy

209F Pati de les Aigües 1987

Carrer Roger de Llúria/carrer Consell de Cent

C. Ribas, Andreu Arriola, Ajuntament de Barcelona, Servei de Projectes Urbans

M Girona, Passeig de Gràcia

The decoration is tastefuly done, and this park allows a rare view of the *inside* of a typical *Eixample* block. Unlike the generally grandiose display of architecture to the street, the backs are very mundane: the ubiquitous residences above the ground floor are almost entirely covered in balconies, many of them fully glazed. The restored water tower now rises from a small lake fed by a fountain which runs along the north wall while the remainder of the square is paved.

210Jf Parc, carrer de la Palla 1988–90

Carrer de la Palla

Luisa Agnado, Ajuntament de Barcelona, Ambit d'Urbanisme i Serveis Municipals, Dte. Ciutat vella

M Liceu

This is probably the smallest park of the programme. A tiny clearing in the dense fabric of the Ciutat vella has been paved with incised marble, and protected by a very refined screen with handsome gates and a rhetorical open canopy in stainless and mild steel.

211I Extension to Montjuïc stadium 1988–90

Montjuïc

Gregotti associates, Frederic Correa i Ruiz, Alfonso Milà, Carles Buxadé, Joan Margerit

Ⓜ Espanya

The original stadium on the site was designed by Pere Domènech on the occasion of Barcelona's unsuccessful bid to host the 1936 Olympic Games. Gregotti associates won the competition for the layout of the whole site for the 1992 Olympics, and the commission to convert the existing stadium. The scheme preserves much of the original neo-classical masonry shell which has been painted a uniform brown. The new work included excavating the arena to a depth of 11 metres to make room for more spectators, increasing the capacity to 70,000, and erecting an elegant steel roof whose plan subtly follows the slight curve of the stadium wall and which cantilevers 30 metres to cover the northern stand.

212I Palau d'Esports Sant Jordi (Arena) 1986–90

Montjuïc

Arata Isozaki

Ⓜ Espanya

In an extraordinary act of faith, the competition for the design of this new arena was announced before Barcelona had submitted its bid to host the 1992 Olympic Games. There are two problems inherent in the design of any such building. First, there is a disparity of scale between the engineering (the roof and seating structures) and the architecture of foyers and circulation, and second, the parts which are the responsibility of the two professions have to be fitted together. In the arena, engineering predominates and the interior is as impressive as any space which seated 17,000 people would be. Seen from outside, the roof sits on a platform of decorated architecture whose wavy roofs distract from the engineering rather than enhancing it. The profile of the main roof seems strangely unresolved, and the banal and small-scaled rooflights which pepper the very top of the dome compromise the heroic engineering. The sculpture on poles outside the building and facing the promenade is by A. Miyawaki.

Post-Franco and democracy

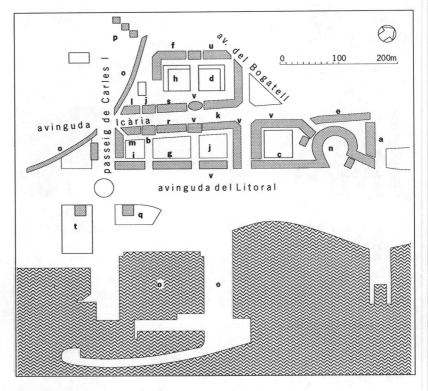

213K **Nova Icària, Olympic village** 1988–

*Planners: MBMP (Martorell Bohigas Mackay
Puigdomenech); various architects*

Ⓜ Ciutadella

Next to the Mediterranean and immediately to the
north east of the Parc de la Ciutadella, the 'village'
was developed on land formerly occupied by de-
caying warehouses and industry. It provides housing for the visiting athletes, coaches and officials
of the 1992 Olympic Games; offices; a hotel and
conference centre; new infrastructure including a
length of the coastal motorway; a marina and two
new beaches.

MBMP's exemplary and sensible plan proposed
extending the passeig de Carles I south to the sea
where the new Olympic marina was sited. On either
side of this axis, and to north and south of the
extended avinguda Icària which connects the
Cimentiri de l'Est to the Passeig de Colom, the new
housing is arranged in a pattern which extends
Cerdà's grid, but amalgamates each three blocks
into one 'superblock'. The housing on each of the

a	Alemany & Poblet
b	Bach & Mora
c	Bonell & Ruis
d	Bonet Castellana
e	Bosch, Tarrús & Vives
f	Cantellops
g	Clotet
h	Compta, Araña & Mora
i	Correra & Milá
j	Domenech, Amado
k	Giraldez, Subias & Lopez
l	Godina, Urgell & Laviña
m	Llimona & R. Valles
n	Martinez, Lapeña & Torres
o	MBMP
p	Mitjans & Ribas Piera
q	Ortiz & Lèon
r	Puig Torner
s	Sanmarti
t	SOM
u	Taller d'Arquitectura Bofill
v	Viaplana & Piñon

resulting parcels of land was designed by various (mostly Catalan) architects, within planning guidelines about form, height and materials. The flats generally follow the perimeter of the blocks, but the large spaces inside the blocks are filled with various experiments in different forms of housing. The two long curved blocks of flats to the south west are by Martorell, Bohigas and Mackay and follow the line of a railway track.

The coastal motorway was put underground where it passes the village, and its roof used as part of a new park between the housing and the sea. The crossing of motorway and the passeig de Carles I is marked by two towers: the Torre Mapfre (architects Iñigo Ortiz and Enrique Lèon) to the east contains offices, and that to the west with its exposed steel frame, the Hotel de les Arts, is by SOM Chicago.

214B Parc della Creuta del Coll 1988

Vallcarca

Josep M. Martorell i Codina, David Mackay Goodchild

In the unlikely setting of an abandoned quarry, this is a successful attempt to design a popular park. The unifying feature is a large circle with which all the other elements engage, or to which they are connected. Most of the the parts are conventional: terraces for parading set into the hillside, an area for bowls, a minimalist pergola, a grove of palms and two interconnected lakes. The light fittings are unusually and mercifully reticent. The Basque sculptor Eduard Chillida's work *In Praise of Water* is suspended above the upper lake, and the tapering struts in Cor-ten steel at the entrance to the park are by Ellsworth Kelly.

215 ONCE kiosk (Organización Nacional de Ciegos España) 1988

Antoni Roselló, Ajuntament de Barcelona, Ambit d'Urbanisme i Serveis Municipals

These ubiquitous cheerful blue 'buildings' sell lottery tickets, and are among a series of new standard designs produced by the Ambit d'Urbanisme for the more common items of street furniture. The kiosks provide shelter for their occupant, so qualifying as architecture, and they provide the time, making them appliances.

Post-Franco and democracy

216Jj Passeig del Moll de la Fusta 1988–89

Passeig del Moll de la Fusta

Manuel de Solà-Morales de Rosselló

M Drassanes/Barceloneta

The citizens of Barcelona had always been separated from the Mediterranean by its walled port, and in the twentieth century increasingly by the traffic on the coastal road. The gradual disuse of the inner harbour and the building of a modern port to the west allowed Barcelona to develop a connection. The ambitious and thoughtful re-ordering of the passeig de Colom was part of a much larger plan to develop Barcelona's system of main roads including the upgrading of the coastal road to a motorway, and the building of the outer ring road which now skirts the base of the mountains to the north-west. The passeig de Colom was rearranged for local traffic as a 'promenade' decorated with palm trees. One carriageway of the coast road was placed in a tunnel, and the former broad quay was re-paved and planted. The roof of the road and an accompanying car park were paved to make a broad walk equipped with tiled benches and pergolas, and this walk was connected to the quay by two elegant red drawbridges which can be lifted to allow the passage of vehicles with tall loads on the road below. The only new buildings were the three pavilions, the one at the eastern end, the restaurant and bar *Gambrinus*, decorated with a large smiling lobster by artist Javier Mariscal on its roof.

Work which will extend access for pedestrians continues at either end of the Passeig de Colom both to improve the junction with the Ramblas at plaça Portal de la Pau, and at the eastern end to connect it with Nova Icària **212**.

217l INEFC, Institut Nacional d'Educació Fisica de Catalunya (sports university) 1988–91

L'Anella Olímpica, Montjuïc

Taller de Arquitectura Bofill

M Espanya

Terminating the axis of the promenade established to the west of the Olympic stadium, the newly established sports university houses spaces for academic and sporting activities. These are arranged round two cloisters with glazed roofs between which is an auditorium. The whole building is clad with the Taller's now standard and beautifully manufactured precast concrete lumps. It is unclear whether or not the suggestions of Classical architecture in both the form or the detail are a serious architectural proposal. If they are not a joke, then this building, like the Taller's extension to Barcelona's airport, demonstrates that the entasis of columns, however inconvenient or difficult to manufacture in concrete rather than stone, was a necessary feature of the language, and that its omission calls the whole enterprise into question.

218F **Col·legi public *Josep Maria Jujol*** 1989

Riera de Sant Miquel/carrer de Travessera de Gràcia

Jaume Bach i Nuñez, Gabriel Mora i Gramunt

F Gràcia M Fontana

The compression of this school into its tight urban site continues the tradition established by Goday earlier in the century, although the planning here is less integrated than that of his schools. Three storeys of classrooms are raised one floor above the level of the street and immediately next to it, and their roof used as a playground. Beyond and at the back of the site, the shell of Jujol's Manyach factory has been preserved and serves as a covered playground .

219B **Telecommunications tower** 1989–91

Turo de Vilana, Collserola

Foster Associates; engineers: Ove Arup and Partners, CAST

The 288-metre-high tower was built to provide a single mast on which the various antennae for Barcelona's many radio and television stations could be mounted, and to avoid these being placed individually along the mountain ridge. This competition-winning design is in the form of a stayed mast, the shaft fabricated of slip-formed concrete with a triangular plan. Cantilevered and suspended from the mast are fourteen floors of accommodation on which the antennae are mounted.

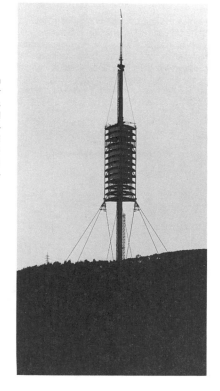

Post-Franco and democracy

220L **Ramblas de Prim** 1989–

Carrer de Prim

Javier San José, Ajuntament de Barcelona, Dte. Sant Martí

M Besós Mar

The sites for the parks programme were even-handedly chosen so that the poorer or less glamorous areas of the city have their share. Here an impossibly wide road lined with undistinguished blocks has been tamed and reordered to provide narrow carriageways for vehicles separated by a wide central reservation for pedestrians. The design of the groundworks is modestly populist, and at present the line of the road is announced vertically only by the obligatory new special lighting

standards. When the laurel and plane trees have grown, however, one of the longest linear parks in the city will have been established. It is planned to extend the new Ramblas to the north, crossing the Gran Via and stopping at the railway; and to the south as far as the sea shore.

221 Ja **Museu d'Art Contemporani (Museum of Contemporary Art), project** 1990–

Carrer dels Angels/carrer Montalegre

Richard Meier and Partners

M Catalunya

A large part of the Caritat district including the site of the old Casa de Misericordia is being redeveloped around a line of three new pedestrian squares, each with its own character. The southerly square was lined with some new housing and completed for use as a neighbourhood park in 1990, and the site for the new museum lies between the two

northerly squares. A new pedestrian route connecting them passes through the museum and is marked with a drum. The entrance is on the south side next to this route, and the main galleries extend north-east from it. The composition disposes the various functions on either side of a central wall which runs the length of the building, projecting at each end and above the roofs. Rooms with particular functions are projected beyond and set against a second wall to the south and parallel to it. This assemblage provides the façade to the north side of the new square and faces the flank of the restored former chapel of the Convent dels Angels on the south.

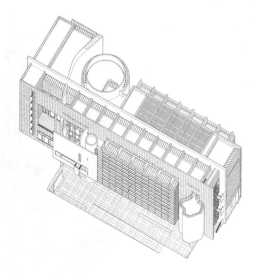

222C Camp de Tir (archery range) 1990–92

Area Olympica Vall d'Hebron

Enric Miralles, Carme Pinós

M Montbau

Four main sites were developed or improved for the 1992 Olympic games and this one, south of the Velòdrom **203**, was laid out as a new sports centre with a covered sports hall, 15-kilometre cycle track, tennis courts and this archery range which, under construction at the time of writing, promised to be one of the more idosyncratic contributions to the Olympic's architectural programme.

223K Teatre Nacional, project 1992–

Taller d'Arquitectura Bofill

Auditori i Arxiu Corona d'Aragó, project 1992–

Rafael Moneo

Avinguda de la Meridiana/carrer de Lepant

M Glòries

Since 1844 and 1905 respectively, the Liceu **54** and Palau Mùsica Catalana **117** have served as

Barcelona's only large auditoria. On land previously used by railway sidings and the tracks into the now refurbished l'Etació del Nord, sites have now been found east of carrer Lepant and south of carrer de Ribes for two new buildings for performances. The project for the Teatre Nacional, designed by Taller Bofill, proposes two buildings in the form of temples at right angles to each other. The design for the Auditori i Arxiu Corona d'Aragó on the site to the west is by Rafael Moneo. The start of both buildings is delayed while the various authorities discuss the arrangements for funding and running them.

224E Offices, shops and flats *Super-illa Diagonal-Winterthur* 1991–

Avinguda Diagonal/carrer Numancia/carrer Entença

Manuel de Solà-Morales de Rosselló, Rafael Moneo

M Les Corts

A gigantic development outside the grid of the *Eixample*, but its length the equivalent of three of its blocks, a 'superblock'. To avinguda Diagonal the single building presents a continuous façade whose roofline varies between seven and fourteen storeys and whose profile in plan has shallow stepped modelling. The elevations are composed entirely of a regular grid of square windows set in a field of masonry.

Colònia Güell, Crypt chapel 1898–1915: exterior 401

Interiors and excursions

300Je **Hotel España** 1902–3

Carrer de Sant Pau, 9–11

Lluís Domènech i Muntaner, Eusebi Arnau

M Liceu

Domènech coordinated this lavish exercise in interior design including the bar to the right of the entrance with its marble fireplace by Arnau, and the dining room with exquisite tilework decorated with sunflowers. The magnificent ballroom, furthest from the entrance and below the patio from which the hotel rooms are reached, is decorated with murals with an underwater theme by Ramon Casas. Domènech also supplied the wall decoration for the flight of stairs between the ground and first floors.

301Jf **Café de l'Opéra**

La Rambla, 74

M Liceu

Barcelona's quintessential bohemian café is as popular with locals as with tourists, impossible to date but its wall decoration appears roughly contemporary with that of that of Goday's schools.

302F **Bar restaurant** *Tictactoe*

Carrer de Roger de Lluria, 40

M Passeig de Gràcia

An over-ripe compendium of kitsch and camp motifs and usages owing little to its contemporary more straightforward post-modernism: the surprise is that the designer has had no idea of when to stop.

Interiors

Much of the craftsmanship which the architects of *Modernisme* could command is still available and Catalan architects and designers were quick to exploit it in the years of liberation after 1975. The following is a selection of Barcelona's extraordinary range of interior spaces all of which are publicly accessible, although some of the bars may charge admission, and some may already have been swept away.

Interiors and excursions

303F   Grocery shop and restaurant *Gran Colmado*

Carrer Consell de Cent, 658

M Passeig de Gràcia

The very long shop leads to a small restaurant (with excellent food) at the rear. The shop has a glass floor, now attractively worn, and the shopfitting, like the merchandise, is of very high quality.

304F   Shoe shop *Eleven*

Avinguda Diagonal, 464

M Diagonal

The sale area is on the first floor reached from the street by a lift with glass sides or an intimidatingly steep ramp. No shoes are displayed at street level, but videos suggest their presence upstairs where they are offered for sale in a mélange of neo-brutalist decoration.

305F   Club *Nick Havanna*

Carrer de Rosello, 208

M Diagonal

One of the earliest clubs to embrace the full decorative repertoire of post-modernism. Its plan is the standard one for the Eixample: a narrow entrance leads to the large bar and disco (dominated by a large pendulum) situated in the middle of the block. The bar staff wear uniforms designed by Jean-Paul Gaultier.

306F   Club *Universal*

Carrer de Marià Cubi, 182–4

M Gràcia

A cool interior with a bar on each of two levels. The lower one with its double height and raw granolithic flooring has the air of a recently disused garage.

307F   Bar restaurant *Casa Fernandez*

Carrer Santalò, 46

F Muntaner

A busy and fashionable tapas bar designed without sentiment for a proprietor who brews his own beer, his brewery master heroically depicted in the mural behind the bar. The restaurant is in a room at the back where diners eat at a single large communal table.

Excursions

The following list is a selection of some of the noteworthy buildings which lie outside Barcelona's city limits. The entries include both works by architects who practised mainly in Barcelona and which illuminate their careers, and others which supplement the history of particular architectural movements.

Advice on routes, public transport and opening times if any may be had from the Catalan tourist office, Direcció General de Turisme, Generalitat de Catalunya, passeig de Gràcia, 105.

400 Wine cellar, house and chapel Güell
1888–90

Carretera Comarcal, 246, Garraf
on the main coast road C246 between
Barcelona and Sitges, about 4 kms from Sitges
Francesc Berenguer i Mestres

Neither house nor courtyard are accessible, but
enough can be seen from the road and through the
gate to confirm this as the most pungent work in
Berenguer's very small *œuvre*. The accommodation is arranged under a single roof of beautifully
weathered pale grey stone, its form perhaps a
reminder of a 'primitive hut', which reaches down
to the ground. The wine cellar is at ground level;
above this is the house; and the chapel is at the top
under the apex of the roof. The gatehouse, built
later, contains the gate made of chains supported
from a catenary.

401 Colònia Güell, Crypt Chapel, 1898–1915

Santa Coloma de Cervelló
on the road parallel to the river Llobregat
between Sant Boi de Llobregat and Sant Vincenc
dels Horts

*Francesc Berenguer i Mestres, Antoni Gaudí i
Cornet*

Güell conceived two projects for 'ideal' colonies,
the later at what is now Park Güell 100, the earlier
here at the site of his father's cotton mill at Santa
Coloma. The colony commissioned from Berenguer
was started in 1898 and finished in 1911. It
included a house for the director, over one hundred
houses for workers, a school and schoolhouse, a
social club, and shops, all contained within a simple
axial plan. Gaudí designed the church whose siting
disregards Berenguer's axis and is set apart from
the secular activities at the edge of a small wood.
Its crypt was completed by 1915, but Güell died
in 1918 and the work left unfinished. Jujol continued with the decoration Gaudí had left unfinished,
but most of his additions were subsequently removed.

Working with Joan Rubió, Gaudí designed the
structure of the crypt to carry the substantial load
of the church above. Four central columns lean
inwards and support the central groined brick
vault. Outside these a ring of ten brick piers carry
further vaults, and the outer ring of vaults over the
ambulatory spans between these and the corrugated exterior wall. Some of the pews are original
and to Gaudí's design while others are modern
reproductions, and the stained glass panels in the
polygonal windows are modern replacement of the
originals destroyed during the Civil War. The room
behind the choir contains a model (of doubtful
provenance) of the whole design showing the
church crowned with three parabolic spires, and a
photograph of the upside-down suspension model
used in designing the crypt vault.

While the apparently disorganised geometry of the
chapel is simply described, it is made hard to read
by the addition of the wildly asymmetrical external
stepped ramp (which was to have led to the main
entrance to the church above and which now
provides a canopy shading the crypt's entrance),
and by the extraordinary range of different sorts of
masonry: grey basalt, sandstone rubble, schist,
pink brick and cinders.

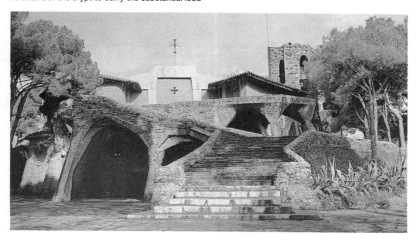

Interiors and excursions

402 Masia Freixa now Escola de Música 1907

Carrer Volta, Terrassa, Vallès occidental
Terrassa is 21kms north west of Barcelona

Lluís Muncunill

Terrassa, with Sabadell, was one of the main centres of the Catalan wool-processing industry, and Muncunill was its municipal architect. This farmhouse formerly used as a factory and now converted to a music school shows him fully aware of the fruitier currents of late *modernista* practice, here combining mudéjar elements like the minaret with a ruthlessly consistent use of the parabolic arch for all the openings.

403 Aymerich i Amat factory now Museu de la Ciència i de la Técnica de Catalunya 1907–10

Rambla d'Egara, Terrassa (see **402**)

Lluís Muncunill

The former factory has been converted into a museum and centre of science and information technology, for which its brick vaulted roof covering an area of 12,000 square metres makes it well suited.

404 Cases Torre de la Creu, 'Torre dels Ous' 1913–16

Carrer de Canalías, 12; Sant Joan Despí, Baix Llobregat
Sant Joan Despí is a small town south west of Barcelona and to the north of the river Llobregat

Josep Maria Jujol i Gilbert

The geometry of the plan—five interpenetrating circles—disguises the fact that this is a pair of semi-detached houses divided by a straight party wall which slices axially through the cylinders. The picturesque silhouette is provided by the the various 'rude' chimneys, and the squashy cornice above which rise the various mosaic-covered domes crowning the cylinders, some of them baroque, others in the form of mushroom caps. The Jujol who designed the balcony fronts to the Casa Milá **119** is evident here in the fine metalwork of the railings to the street.

405 Casa Negre 1914–30

Torrent del Negre, 37; Sant Joan Despí, Baix Llobregat
Sant Joan Despí is a small town south west of Barcelona and to the north of the river Llobregat

Josep Maria Jujol i Gilbert

Jujol who was for a time municipal architect of Sant Joan Despí renovated and expanded this earlier country house or *masia*. Unkempt, and facing a small square in the town which has engulfed it, it is now used by the municipality as a cultural centre. Jujol provided the decorative scheme for the entire façade with *esgrafiats in* fawn and cream, and added the central bay window supported on spindly raked iron columns. Inside, the chapel on the second floor and the stair up to it are entirely by Jujol, decorated in a wild mixture of both recognisably historical and novel calligraphic motifs.

406 Església paroquial 1918–23

Vistabella, Tarragona
Vistabella is a small country town 10 kms north of Tarragona which is on the coast 80 kms southwest of Barcelona

Josep Maria Jujol i Gilbert

One of Jujol's rare freestanding works, and not a conversion, the church has a square plan, its axis on the diagonal. The central vault and crowning parabolic dome and pyramidal open belfry are supported by four arches set in from the surrounding square. Jujol was able to complete his lavish scheme for the decoration of the interior which was restored in the 1960s.

407 Sanctuary, Montserrat 1926–31

Montserrat, 35 kms north west of Barcelona on the road to Manresa

Josep Maria Jujol i Gilbert

This abandoned and unfinished ruin is included here as an important work in Jujol's *oeuvre* and because the chapel provides an antidote to the dour unattractiveness of Montserrat's main pilgrimage centre. Portions of the walls together with some vaulting remain: enough to demonstrate the earnestness of Jujol's continuous experiment with novel forms of construction.

408 Casa Jujol 1932

Carrer de Jacint Verdaguer, 31; St Joan Despi, Baix Llobregat. Sant Joan Despí is south west of Barcelona and to the north of the river Llobregat

Josep Maria Jujol i Gilbert

For the architect himself, the accommodation of this simple bungalow which would happily find itself in Los Angeles is organised in two wings at right angles to each other. Like its neighbour it is decorated with blue *esgrafiats* on a white ground.

At carrer de Jacint Verdaguer, 29 Jujol converted an existing house, the **Casa Serra-Xaus** to provide a second home as country retreat and also decorated it with blue *esgrafiats*.

409 Walden 7 1970–75

Sant Just Desvern, 4km west of Barcelona on the road to Sant Feliu de Llobregat and Tarragona.

Taller de Arquitectura Bofill

An alarming and massive essay in mass housing, now a stranded relic of the architectural optimism which supposed that architects could be successful social engineers as well as supplying shelter. The flats are extremely small, their cladding of tiles is being shed like flakes of skin, and its inhabitants very wary of visitors.

The architects' office, recognisable by its decoration of cypress trees, is housed in the converted cement works next door to the block.

410 Railway station 1982

Bellaterra, 15kms north west of Barcelona on the road to Sabadell

Jaume Bach i Nuñez, Gabriel Mora i Gramunt

F from Catalunya

The new station was built at the terminus of the railway line that was extended to serve the Autonomous University of Barcelona (in ominous 1960s concrete) situated in the country across the mountains from Barcelona. The platform side presents a simple marble wall from which a delicate canopy is suspended. The entrance side by contrast offers a simple lean-to punctured by a shallow segmental arch over a flight of steps. To the right of the entrance, three massive counterweights project from the back of the wall to balance the weight of the canopy on the reverse. Photography is discouraged.

411 Cemetery, Igualada 1990–

Igualada is about 50kms west of Barcelona on the road N11 to Lleida

Enric Miralles and Carme Piños

Arranged on a hillside, the first phase of the cemetery includes the triangular mortuary chapel and the first two arms of the Z-shaped arrangement of raked walls of mortuary niches capped with overhanging cornices.

Interiors and excursions

412 Municipal sports hall 1990–92

Badalona, northwest of Barcelona across the river Besòs

Esteve Bonell i Costa and Francesc Rius i Camps

Ⓜ Gorg

In an urban plaça rather than a suburban setting, this is the latest monument to sport from the architects of the magnificent Velodróm d'Horta **204**. The stadium, its bulk reduced by having the pitch sunk well into the ground, seats 12,000 people in two elliptical tiers under a saw-toothed north lit roof. The enclosing walls are extended and broken on the long axis to provide a grand formal entrance, and are topped by a thinly and beautifully detailed loggia which gives views on to the surrounding streets.

Vocabulary: Catalan, Castilian, English

The Catalan language was suppressed during the Franco regime, but since 1975 is now, with Castilian Spanish, one of Catalonia's two official languages. Older maps and guides may use Castilian, but all Barcelona's street signs have been altered to Catalan.

Catalan	Castilian	English
avinguda	avenida	avenue
capella	capilla	chapel
carrer	calle	street
Eixample	Ensanche	expansion (The Cerdá plan)
església	iglesia	church
esgrafiats		incised stucco
illa	manzana	(city) block
mercat	mercado	market
muntanya	montaña	mountain
nou	nuevo	new
palau	palaçio	palace
parc	parque	park
passatge	pasaje	arcade, passage
passeig	paseo	road
pati	patio	courtyard
pla	plano	plan
plaça	plaza	square
poble	pueblo	village
pont	puente	bridge
portal	puerta	gate, door

Illustration acknowledgements

The photographs are by Carmel Lewin and the author with the exception of the following: 141, Katharine Reeve; 145, Spanish National Tourist Office London; 218, Foster Associates; 220, Richard Meier & Partners.

The base map used on pages 154–155 and 156–157 is reproduced with the kind permission of the Institut Municipal d'Informatica, Centre de Cartografia Automàtica, Barcelona.

Index

References to entries are in bold type e.g. **24**
References to items within entries are in plain type: 33
References in italics are to page numbers: *55*

Index

Index

Index

Park Güell 100, retaining wall: Antoni Gaudi i Cornet

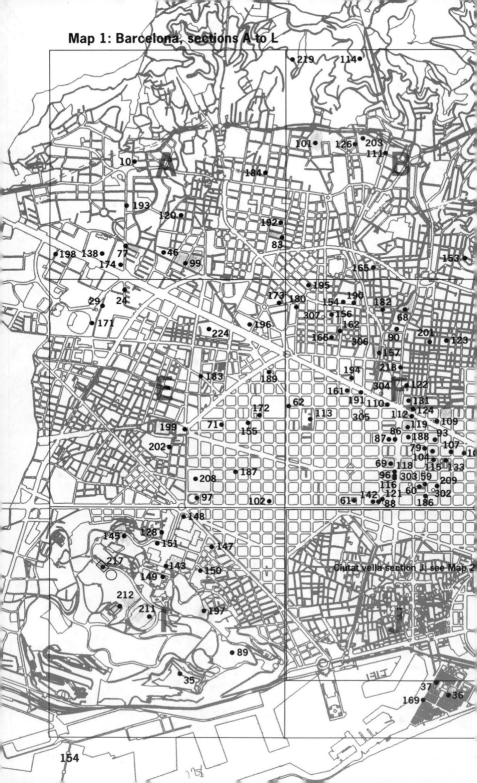

Map 1: Barcelona, sections A to L